A Lifetime of Small Adventures

Stories of Adventure, Misadventure, and
Lessons Learned Along the Way

D1362341

A Lifetime of
Small
Adventures

Stories of Adventure, Misadventure, and Lessons Learned Along the Way

Bill Birnbaum

Douglas Mountain Publishing
Sisters, Oregon

A Lifetime of Small Adventures
Stories of Adventure, Misadventure, and Lessons Learned Along the Way

by Bill Birnbaum

Published by:
Douglas Mountain Publishing
Post Office Box 1570
Sisters, Oregon 97759
Phone: (541) 588-6297

ISBN: 978-1-932632-00-2
LCCN: 2010926419

Book and cover design by Peri Poloni-Gabriel, Knockout Design, www.knockoutbooks.com

Edited by Gail M. Kearns, www.topressandbeyond.com

Publisher's Cataloging-in-Publication
(Provided by Quality Books, Inc.)

Birnbaum, William S.
    A lifetime of small adventures : stories of adventure, misadventure and
lessons learned along the way / Bill Birnbaum.
    p. cm.
    LCCN 2010926419
    ISBN-13: 978-1-932632-00-2
    ISBN-10: 1-932632-00-X
    1. Birnbaum, William S. 2. Business consultants--
Biography. 3. Conduct of life.   I. Title.

HD69.C6B57 2011   001'.092
                                               QBI10-600099

10 9 8 7 6 5 4 3 2 1

Printed in the United States of America

Contents

Dedication

To my brother Larry, with love.
If he had lived past the age of nine,
then he too could have enjoyed
a lifetime of small adventures.

Introduction

MY MOM TURNED AWAY JUST FOR A MOMENT. Then I, as a three-year-old boy, stepped up onto the bus. The doors closed and away I went down 13ᵗʰ Avenue. About that time, Mom discovered I was gone. She hurriedly looked in all directions and screamed, "Billy, where's Billy?"

On that bright, sun shiny morning in the summer of 1945, Mom had taken me along on her shopping trip. Just a couple of blocks from our home, we ran into a lady she knew, so they stopped to chat. While engrossed in conversation, neither of them noticed my walking toward the corner of the block. A bus pulled up right in front of me. Some passengers stepped off the bus; others stepped on. Apparently, this seemed pretty interesting to me, so I too climbed aboard the bus.

As the bus traveled down 13ᵗʰ Avenue, I wandered about the aisle to see whatever I might. Finally realizing that I was in a strange place without my mother, I began to cry. I guess I cried loud enough that the driver turned to see me standing in the aisle. He waived toward me shouting, "Hey, whose kid is that?"

No one answered, so he repeated his question even louder, "Whose kid is that?"

Still, no one answered, so the driver pulled the bus over to the curb and brought it to a stop. He jumped up out of his seat, hurried over to me, and shouted, "Hey, whose kid is this?"

Fortunately, a man on the bus recognized me. He had seen me once or twice in my dad's grocery store. He told the driver, "Oh yes, I know who that boy is. He's Sol Birnbaum's son. His father has the grocery store over on 49th Street. I'll take him to his dad."

And so, I stepped off the bus holding the hand of the man who knew my father. Twenty minutes later, I was in my dad's store drinking a glass of milk. To my delight I'm sure. And to my mother's likely more so.

As far as I know, that ride on the 13th Avenue bus was my very first adventure. But it was hardly my last. For it set the tone for a series of small adventures throughout my lifetime. And that's what this book is about—my lifetime of small adventures.

I've divided this book into five parts. In Part One, I'll relate my adventures as a boy growing up in Brooklyn, New York. You'll read of my flooding the basement of our home, quite accidentally I assure you. And of my interest in chemistry leading to my building bombs, and to my using those bombs to do just a little bit of damage. And of my placing pennies on the railroad tracks so an arriving train would "squirt" each penny off to the side of the track as a projectile, very much like a bullet. And you'll learn that, during my college years, I developed a fondness for picking up hitchhikers. Most of them were OK. Only a couple of times was I in any real danger. All of those activities in pursuit of adventure, of course.

In Part Two, I'll tell of my adventures as a young, single fellow living and working in Southern California. You'll read of my leading climbing trips in California's Sierra Nevada Mountains and in the California Desert. And about a number of my hitchhiking adventures. And about the time when flying at twenty-five hundred feet elevation, our plane's single engine stopped. Yeah, stopped.

In Part Three, I'll share with you two of my special places. The two places where I returned for adventure, again and again. First you'll read about my travels in Baja California, Mexico. Like our towing a twin engine plane out of a dry lakebed. And about the time I sat just behind the pilot when he crash landed on a dirt runway. You'll read also about two armed guards running over to our truck while pointing rifles at us.

Also in Part Three, you'll read of my adventures in "The Place Where Nobody Goes"—a unique spot on the north rim of the Grand Canyon. I'll tell you about my being caught by the current while swimming across the Colorado River—while listening to the sound of the downstream rapids growing louder and louder. And you'll learn about a swell fellow named John Riffy, the ranger who befriended us. And we him.

In Part Four, I'll tell how the arrival of both middle age and fatherhood caused me to reflect. Yep, I actually began to think about life's meanings. I figured out that adventurous activities like climbing mountains are more than just a physical pursuit. I discovered that they also contain intellectual and emotional dimensions.

You'll find that I'm quite opinionated. I'll tell you my thoughts about we creatures of modern society being too damn busy. And too wrapped up in materialism. And, at times, concerned about a bunch of stuff that really isn't important. You'll learn of my thoughts about the dignity of man. And also about "the three ages of man." And you'll read of my own personal experience, far from home and family, on the morning of September 11, 2001.

In Part Five, you'll learn about my senior years (to date, of course, because they're not yet over). I'll tell you about my marrying the "right" woman. A gal who is every bit as crazy for adventure as I am. And about how our quest for adventure led to our buying two one-way tickets to Arequipa, Peru, and flying there in search of volunteer opportunities.

Also in Part Five, you'll learn that I avoid using the word "retirement." Unless of course it's coupled with the word "adventure," as in "adventure retirement."

Welcome to *A Lifetime of Small Adventures*. If there's even a bit of the adventurer in you, you'll love reading this book. ➤

Part One

A Kid in New York

BEING BORN AND RAISED IN BROOKLYN wasn't my idea; it just happened to me. More of a country boy at heart, I didn't like living in the city. Instead, I wanted to live out on Long Island. Ideally in a rural area, like Northport, where Aunt Ruthie and Unk lived. Or Mineola where my grandparents lived.

But we had to live in Brooklyn. Because, as Mom explained each time I raised the subject, "That's where Daddy has his grocery store."

My dad would give me the same answer in slightly different words, "You've got to go where your bread is buttered."

Even though I disliked Brooklyn, I still had some pretty good adventures while living there. Looking back after all these years, it seems to me that some of those adventures might have bordered on misbehavior. Maybe.

Chapter 1

Dad

WHEN MY DAD WAS A BOY, he lived on a farm about a half day's ride from town. So whenever the family needed supplies, his father would hitch the horse to the wagon for the daylong round trip. Sometimes Dad got to go along, an event which he much enjoyed. At the general store in town, they'd buy the needed supplies, load them into the wagon, and begin their return trip home.

During the winter especially, when the days were short, it would turn dark and cold during their ride home. So somewhere along the road, my dad and his would hop into the back of the wagon. There, they'd lie down together, under a blanket, and go to sleep. And the horse, without any human guidance at all, would deliver them back home to their farm.

I think it's remarkable that the horse knew its way back home. And what a wonderful father/son experience. Being transported home while sleeping under a blanket in the back of the wagon. Just the two of them together.

One time, in fact the last time they rode together in the wagon, they weren't alone. My dad's mom was also in the wagon. And so was a cousin. And two neighbors.

They weren't going into town for supplies. Instead, they were running away, because the soldiers had started shooting.

Some months earlier, the soldiers began stealing things, mostly farm animals and crops. More recently, they were hitting people with their rifles. And just a few days earlier, they started shooting. They had killed one of my dad's cousins. And a neighbor too. It was time to leave.

It must have been difficult for the horse with so many people in the wagon. And with the weight of their luggage. And the weight of the silverware and candle sticks and jewelry. These were the treasures they'd sell to pay for their passage. First across Europe by train. Then to England by boat. And finally, on a much larger boat to America.

They sold their first treasure when they arrived at the train station. How must Dad have felt, as a nine-year-old boy, saying goodbye to his beloved horse and wagon?

Dad didn't tell me much about the train ride across Europe. Except that it was terribly cold. And that their clothing wasn't sufficient to keep them warm, so they stuffed newspaper between their inner and outer garments. And they shivered a lot.

On the boat from England to America, they sailed through a terrible storm. Dad said that the waves got up to sixty feet high.

Gee, I don't know about that. Sixty feet? How did he know the waves were that high? After all, he and his family were down in the bottom of the boat. Steerage, I think it's called. Rich people got to ride up at the deck level. But poor people had to stay below in steerage.

Dad and his family were now poor. Back home on their farm, they had owned a lot of land. Land that would now remain fallow. And they had owned many animals. Animals that the soldiers would soon slaughter. And they had lived in a very large house. A house that the Russian government would soon turn into a military headquarters, and later into a regional post office.

Dad said that lots of people down in steerage were sick throughout the entire voyage. Seems to me that if the sea were so terribly rough it would be better to be above deck. That way, you could look out toward the horizon. I think that would be somewhat reassuring. But crowded in steerage below, with the boat rocking this way and that, it must have been awful.

I wonder how much Dad and his family knew about America. Certainly they knew that Americans spoke a different language. But did they know much more? Had they heard tales of opportunity and riches for all? Maybe. One thing for sure—they knew that, in America, soldiers didn't steal things from people, or hit people with rifles, or shoot people, just because those people were of a different religion.

Algodón

During the early 1950s, supermarkets were becoming a major force in the grocery industry. The dominant supermarket chain in New York City was the A&P—growing fast and driving out the independent grocers one after another. At the time, my dad owned and operated a grocery store in Brooklyn, New York. Like most independent grocers, he worked long and hard to eke out a modest living.

One block away from Dad's store, the A&P opened a new supermarket. Predictably, my dad's business suffered immediately. In fact, it looked as if he'd have to close up shop. But then something really interesting happened.

My mom, both my brothers, and I happened to be there when a small olive-skinned boy walked into Dad's store. I was nine or ten at the time and this kid looked a couple of years younger.

He stepped up to my dad and said just one word, "algodón." Without having the slightest idea of the meaning of the word, Dad repeated, "algodón."

And the boy replied, "Sí, algodón."

As Mom, my brothers and I all looked on, Dad began a game of trial and error. He presented, one at a time, a can of this, a jar of that, an egg, an onion, and a loaf of Wonder Bread. Seems that none of that stuff was algodón.

Then Dad invited the boy to look all around the store for algodón. But the boy just stared at him blankly.

Watching the two of them getting nowhere, I figured that this encounter would end in mutual disappointment. But Mom surprised us all. How in the world she ever figured it out, I don't know. She walked over to the shelf behind the check stand and took down a box of Johnson & Johnson surgical cotton. She showed it to the boy whose expression changed just enough that we were all encouraged. Mom then opened the box exposing the end of the roll of cotton.

Suddenly, a big smile appeared across the boy's face. And through that smile, he said, "Sí, algodón."

The boy dug into the pocket of his jeans and pulled out a dollar bill. He handed the bill to Dad who then gave him his change and the box of cotton in a small paper bag. Dad said, "Thank you."

The boy smiled and turned for the door. We all waved goodbye.

I thought this was all pretty neat. I mean with Mom having saved the day. All's well that ends well, I figured. And besides, I had just learned my first Spanish word: algodón means cotton.

That's what I learned. But Dad learned a whole lot more. For he realized that this incident with the young boy was a sign of things to come. You see, at the same time that the A&P was knocking out the independent grocers, a significant demographic change was taking place. Puerto Rican people were beginning to immigrate into New York City. And as luck would have it, Dad's store was right in the middle of a neighborhood into which these folks were moving.

Dad recognized this as an opportunity. I'm sure he'd never heard the term "niche market," but that didn't slow him down in the least. He found importers who'd supply tropical fruits and vegetables. He bought rice in hundred pound sacks. And he got Del Monte and Hunt Foods to deliver canned goods with Spanish language labels.

It seemed like overnight Dad learned to speak Spanish. The way I remember it, on Tuesday morning he couldn't speak a word and by Friday evening he was fluent. He hired two helpers, Geraldo and Carlos, both recent arrivals from Puerto Rico. And Dad had all of his signs, both inside and outside his store, printed in Spanish. Through all of these changes, Dad made his Puerto Rican customers feel *en su casa* (right at home) in his store.

Dad's decision to specialize made him successful. Oh, I don't mean financially successful, for he never made a lot of money. But he did lift us up into the middle class. And by doing so, he accomplished his one and only personal objective. That his sons would get a college education. So they, unlike he, would work with their minds instead of their hands.

You know something? Even today, after all these years, if I happen to read or hear the word algodón, I smile.

Unk

My mom's sister Ruth and her husband Ed lived in the Village of Northport on Long Island's north shore. With a population of some 3,500 people, Northport seemed to me the prettiest place on the island. Not just pretty, it was also a place where a boy could find much adventure. An old barn in the woods, well on its way toward deterioration, leaned over like the Tower of Pisa. Except that it housed a bunch more spider webs and mouse droppings than the famous tower.

The Northport Hardware Store sold bamboo fishing poles for just twenty-five cents. So a kid could well afford to walk out onto the dock, thread a worm on a hook, and spend the morning staring at the surface of the water. On many summer mornings, I dropped my line into the water and waited anxiously for that telltale nibble.

And there were the beaches. Ashroken, Sand City, Crab Meadow—all offering hot sand, horseshoe crabs, and calm water—perfect for a cool swim on a warm summer's day.

I loved Northport and I loved Aunt Ruthie and Unk, so I spent much of my vacation time living with them. As Unk was a high school teacher, and I a student, we had similar vacation schedules. So he and I spent lots of time together.

Aunt Ruthie and Unk had no children of their own. So my spending time with them added an additional dimension to their lives. Perhaps my staying with them in Northport was as good for them as it was for me. At least I like to think it was. I recall my mom once telling me, "Billy, you're a very lucky boy. For not many boys have two sets of parents."

Unk had two boats, an outboard powered ski boat and a two-person kayak. Most summer morning's he'd ask me, "Billy, which boat should we take out today?"

My answer was always the same, "Let's take the kayak."

Of course, we'd first have to do our chores. Aunt Ruthie worked from nine to five as office manager for the local fuel oil company. So Unk and I did the grocery shopping plus all the chores around the house. Chores completed, we could then spend the rest of the day as we pleased—till five o'clock when Aunt Ruthie finished work.

Aunt Ruthie enjoyed walking to work in the morning. It was about a mile down the hill to her office at the harbor. As she was without a car, Unk and I picked her up at the end of the workday. Following work, she generally chose to go for a swim at Ashroken Beach. On those occasions, we returned the kayak to the house, picked up Aunt Ruthie at her office, then drove back to the beach.

Occasionally, Aunt Ruthie chose to go waterskiing. So Unk and I launched the ski boat late in the afternoon. Then I'd wait at the beach with the boat while Unk drove back to the village to pick up Aunt Ruthie.

Early in our kayaking career, Unk decided that he liked sitting up front. Coincidently, I preferred to sit in the rear. So we never had to rethink our seating arrangement. We'd hop aboard and begin paddling around Huntington Bay. Then, after a while, we might explore some of the inlets and coves—like Duck Island and the adjacent mud flats. Then back out to the bay. Whenever we felt like taking a rest, we'd stop paddling and just kind of drift along relaxing in the warm summer sun.

Unk taught social studies, so he knew all sorts of interesting facts. And he was good at creating test questions. Right there in the middle of our warm, restful drift, he might ask me to name all of the states of the United States and their capital cities. He'd have me name them in some specific order, like clockwise around the country beginning with the State of Maine. I was then to fill in all of the remaining states beginning with those bordering the Mississippi River. Thanks to Unk, I got pretty good at U.S. geography.

A couple of times, Unk asked me, "Billy, can you list, in chronological order, each of the U.S. presidents and vice-presidents, plus the year they entered office?"

I'd respond, "Gosh, no Unk. I'm sure I could hardly get started with that list."

He'd reply, "OK, let's see if I can do it."

And he'd do it—all the way from Washington-Adams in 1789 to Eisenhower-Nixon in 1953. I listened politely, but to tell you the truth, I was hardly paying attention. If Unk happened to make a mistake with Warren G. Harding's vice-president or his first year in office, I really wouldn't know it.

Before long, we might feel like going for a swim. So we'd paddle over to the shore, drag the kayak up onto the sand, and dive into the water. We'd swim around for twenty minutes or so, then go back to kayaking.

After a while, we'd return to drifting lazily. I remember once, while drifting along quietly, I was overcome by a feeling of sadness. I said, "I wish my dad could be here with us."

Unk replied, "Your dad has to work in his store."

"Yes, I know. He sure works a lot," I said.

Then Unk explained what I already knew. "Your dad works as many hours as he does because he didn't have benefit of an education. As an immigrant whose parents died when he was still a teenager, he had to work at a very early age. It's his lack of education that forces him to work as hard as he does. And as many hours as he does. You understand that, don't you Billy?"

"Yes Unk, I understand." ➤

Chapter 2

Grandpa

MY MOM'S HOMETOWN is the Long Island village of Mineola, New York. The town had a population of about thirty-five thousand when I was a kid. While I was growing up, my grandparents—my mom's folks—lived there, so we visited quite often.

I recall, when I was about four, walking down Mineola's Main Street holding my grandfather's hand. About every twenty feet along the sidewalk, or so it seemed, someone would greet Grandpa, "Good morning, Mr. Greenstein." I remember thinking that was so neat. Seemed that everyone along Main Street knew grandpa. I figured that he was so very important. And maybe I was important too because I was his grandson.

Grandpa was born in Austria Hungary about 1887. He came to America as a three-year-old child when his family settled in New York City. Grandma too came from Austria Hungary, also as a child. After they married, they moved slowly east out onto Long Island. First they lived in Brooklyn, and that's where Uncle George was born. Then they lived in Queens and that's where my mom was born. Finally they moved to Mineola, and that's where Aunt Ruthie was born.

The reason why everyone along Main Street knew Grandpa was because, for many years, he had his store on Main Street. My folks had a photo of Grandpa and Uncle George standing in front of Grandpa's store, "Harry's Busy Corner." Judging by Uncle George's apparent age in the photo, it was taken about 1915.

By the time I was born in December of 1941, Grandpa had moved a few blocks down Main Street and was then operating his uniform business from the storefront of his home. It seemed really neat to me that he could be right there at home and yet ready to serve a customer should one come through the front door of his shop.

In his store, Grandpa sold all sorts of uniforms. He had uniforms for nurses, policeman, maids, and butlers. He even sold policemen's night sticks. In fact, when Grandpa wasn't looking, I would play with the nightsticks. I thought it would be cool if Grandpa also sold guns, but I suppose that guns weren't part of the police uniform.

Local customers came into his store to purchase uniforms. Especially the officers from the Mineola Police Force and the nurses from the Nassau County Hospital.

But Grandpa also had some accounts that he would occasionally visit. Like hospitals and police departments in nearby towns. He'd get in his old Dodge coupe, light up his pipe, and drive up Mineola Boulevard onto Jericho Turnpike. So while Grandma minded the store for the day, Grandpa drove around visiting his accounts.

The Russian Embassy

Once in a while, Grandpa invited me along on his customer visits. And I, of course, always jumped at the opportunity. Because it sounded like fun and because I simply loved going places with Grandpa.

Once, when I was about six years old, Grandpa had to drive out to the Russian Embassy in Old Westbury. The embassy purchased uniforms for their maids, butlers, cooks, and waiters. Since I was only six years old,

I had no idea what an embassy was. But that didn't matter. A new word suggested an adventure so I made a run for the car.

I'm not sure what's going on in Old Westbury today, but back when I was a kid, the town contained a bunch of old mansions. As my mom explained, "Old Westbury meant Old Money." Rich folks on multiple-acre estates. The Russian government had purchased one of those estates to use as their embassy.

Grandpa drove the old Dodge coupe up to the giant front gate where a guard asked us why we were there. Grandpa explained that he had an appointment with a particular man. The guard stepped into a small building that looked like an oversized telephone booth. He picked up a piece of paper from his desk, studied it for just a few seconds, and then swung the gate open.

Grandpa said, "Thank you," and drove through the open gate.

I don't know how far we drove once past the gate, but it seemed a very long way. I remember the tree-lined road with branches arching above like we were driving through a tunnel of leaves. Finally, there was the house over to the right side of the road.

Oh my gosh, I thought. *It was a giant house and ever so beautiful!*

As we drove up to the house, a man in a uniform came scurrying down the long flight of stairs. And when Grandpa brought the old Dodge coupe to a stop, the man opened the passenger door for me. He said "hello" as I stepped down from the car.

Grandpa and I walked up the stairs toward the very large entry door and, there, another man opened the door for us. He too said "hello."

Once inside, a third man greeted us and showed us into a giant room containing a very large desk. This third man was the one with whom Grandpa was to meet. They would talk about the embassy buying some uniforms.

The man asked Grandpa if he might offer me some milk and cookies.

Grandpa said that would be OK. I too thought it would be OK. Then the man pushed a button on his desk and, almost immediately, a lady dressed in white came into the room. I was to follow her and she'd give me milk and cookies. Actually, I was a bit nervous about being away from Grandpa in such a strange place, but he gave me a reassuring nod and that made it OK. So off we went, the lady in white and I.

Turns out that she was dressed in white because she was a cook. She took me into the kitchen where there were another three or four ladies also dressed in white. The kitchen was the most remarkable place I'd ever seen. Up till then, the only kitchens I'd ever seen were in people's houses. Kitchens with white porcelain sinks, Formica counters, and the like.

Well, this kitchen was nothing like that. This was a full commercial kitchen. The kind they have in large restaurants and hotels. This place was loaded with stainless steel. And it was huge!

I suppose not that many six-year-old boys visit the kitchen in the Russian Embassy. At least they didn't in those days, as the ladies in white made quite a fuss over me. They sat me up on one of the stainless steel counters and gave me the promised milk and cookies. Then one of them remembered that they also had some cake. So cake appeared as well. And then some ice cream.

I was about half finished with my cake and ice cream when the telephone rang. The man who was meeting with Grandpa was calling for me to return to his office because their meeting had ended. The lady who had earlier taken me to the kitchen walked with me back to the office where Grandpa was waiting. He was ready to leave.

Grandpa and I walked down the long flight of steps where the same man again opened the passenger door for me. Then he hurried around to the other side of the car and opened the door for Grandpa. We drove out through the tunnel of leaves. And that concluded my visit to the Russian Embassy.

In 1959, more than a full decade later, Nikita Khrushchev, then the Premier of Russia, visited New York to address the United Nations. During that visit, he stayed at the Russian Embassy in Old Westbury. His visit was well covered by the press. One evening, while alone watching the news on television, I saw some reporters driving up to the gates of the embassy. The television camera was mounted inside the car so the television audience could see out in front, just as if they were a passenger in the car. The scene looked exactly like it did riding in Grandpa's old Dodge coupe many years earlier.

Right there on the television news program, the embassy gate swung open. The car entered through the gate and drove down a tree-lined road with branches arching above. It was just like driving through a tunnel of leaves. The car pulled up in front of a large beautiful house. And there, a man came running down the steps to meet the car.

I jumped up from the couch and shouted, "Yes, that's it! That's exactly as it was. I remember. I was there with my grandpa."

Grandpa's Safe

Behind the counter in his uniform store, Grandpa had a large combination safe. Perhaps three feet tall by two and a half feet wide by two and a half feet deep— like the safes you see in the cowboy movies. You know, the kind the robbers shoot open with their six-shooters.

Grandpa kept the safe open all the time because he didn't know the combination. Were he to close the safe, he wouldn't be able to open it again. He kept his cash register on top of the safe and some non-valuable papers within. So the safe served not really as a safe, but as a cabinet.

As I understood it, Grandpa never did have the combination to the safe. I think he bought it in an "as is" condition. The safe's lock was in the "locked" position—that is, the bolt was extended out from the open door. This was good, for it meant that the door to the safe couldn't swing closed and accidentally lock.

One rainy morning, when I was about ten years old, I sat on the floor in front of the safe. I placed my ear against the safe's door and turned the combination lock's handle back and forth, listening all the while. Heck no, I didn't know what I was doing. But I had seen this exact thing done by someone or another in a movie. So I figured I should listen for some unusual sound.

In that movie, a safecracker turned the knob first one way, then the other. So that's what I figured I'd do. But which way to start turning? And how many turns? I had no idea. But I got pretty engrossed in the process so, hour after hour, I sat there turning and listening.

I didn't know if it were my imagination or not, but I thought I heard a sound like a piece of metal falling into place. When I heard the sound, I wrote down both the direction I had been turning the dial and the number on it. Then I reversed the direction of turning and listened for the sound to repeat. All the while, I turned the knob ever so slowly.

Toward the middle of the afternoon, both Grandma and Grandpa came by to encourage me to quit what I was doing. Earlier in the day, they seemed pleased that I had found something to keep me out of trouble on a rainy morning. But after five or six hours of turning and listening, they began to express a bit of worry about their oldest grandchild.

But I kept turning and I kept listening and, would you believe it? About 5:00 PM, after an entire day of turning, listening, and writing down directions of turns and numbers on the dial, I had unlocked the safe. Oh my gosh! I jumped for joy. I had cracked the safe just like the bad guys do in the movies!

I guess I was doing quite a bit of shouting, because before I could even think to call them in, Grandma and Grandpa came running into the room. Not only was I pretty darn proud of myself, but I also figured that I did Grandpa a giant favor. Now he could lock his safe and use it as a real safe as well as a cabinet to support his cash register.

I'm not really sure why, but Grandma and Grandpa were both far less enthusiastic about my accomplishment than I was. In fact, they expressed some concern. They worried a bit about their grandchild who, at the age of ten, had just cracked a safe. That was their spoken concern.

I think too they also had an unspoken concern. I didn't figure this out right away, but after some years of thinking about it, I believe that both Grandma and Grandpa had been quite satisfied with their un-locking safe. For even though they now had the combination to the safe, they never did use it as a safe. They continued to keep the door open in the "locked" position and to use the safe as a cabinet.

Though Grandpa's was the one and only safe I ever cracked, I'm still darn proud of my accomplishment. Sometimes in a social gathering, like at a cocktail party, a wedding, or an association meeting, I look around the room and think, *I'm probably the only accomplished safecracker in this entire room.* ➤

Chapter 3

The Mineola Railroad Station

IN MY EARLIEST MEMORY of the Mineola railroad station, I was about four years old, standing on the station platform holding my grandfather's hand. Grandpa had taken me to the station to watch the trains coming and going, which, in those days, was really an exciting event. Back then, in the 1940s, the locomotives were steam driven.

With the train stopped at the station, passengers stepped down from the train and walked to the stationhouse or to their car in the parking lot. Then the conductor shouted "all aboard," and a new crop of passengers stepped aboard the train. The engine then made a loud hissing sound, and a whole bunch of steam spewed from under and over the locomotive.

Slowly the train started forward, the drive rods pushing the enormous wheels round and round. Chug. Chug. Chug. As the locomotive passed by, we could see the fireman shoveling coal into the boiler. The train moved ever so slowly at first. Then faster and faster. The choo, choo, choo sounds now much closer together. Finally, the train became quieter, and seemingly smaller, as it rolled away toward the horizon.

Once, while standing on the station platform holding Grandpa's hand, I heard a whistle off in the distance. A train was coming. Grandpa said that the whistle meant that the train wouldn't be stopping in Mineola. This was an express train that would go right on by at high speed. Grandpa said the safest thing for us to do would be to back away from the tracks. He suggested that we stand way back by the stationhouse.

But I wanted to stand closer. So grandpa and I had quite a discussion about how close we should stand. We ended up with sort of a compromise. We stood about in the middle of the platform, about halfway between the tracks and the stationhouse. Then came another whistle, this one considerably louder than the first. The train was coming closer.

And then we could see the train. It was approaching fast! And it was loud! Then came the screech of another whistle as the train flew by the station platform at an enormous speed. All of a sudden, I became terrified! So I pulled free from Grandpa's hand and went running away from the tracks. By the time Grandpa caught up with me, I was hiding behind the stationhouse.

As the years passed, I found many places to play in Mineola, but the railroad station remained my favorite because it was loaded with adventure. The station was split by a set of double tracks (westbound and eastbound) into north and south side platforms. The ticket office and waiting room were on the north side platform. But the south side platform was far more interesting. On it stood a small wooden building that served as a waiting room. It also served as a warming shed, for right in the middle of the building was a potbellied stove.

This warming shed was an especially fun place during the winter months. During the winter, six or eight elderly men would sit for hours on wooden chairs, huddled around the potbellied stove. They'd tell stories, chew tobacco, and best of all, they'd spit tobacco juice on the hot stove. I loved to listen to their stories about how things were different—generally better—before Harry Truman was president. And what it was like to drive out to Suffolk County when Jericho Turnpike was still a dirt road.

I'd remain attentive for the next spit of tobacco juice because I loved the sound, sight, and smell of tobacco on the hot stove. The old timers seemed to tolerate me. They let me sit there and listen, and watch.

I spent most of the summer of my twelfth year at my grandparent's home in Mineola.

About twice each week, generally over breakfast, Grandma would suggest that I play with Robbie and Jeff Culver, who lived a couple of blocks away, over near the post office. Robbie was a year older than I, and Jeff about a year younger. They were really nice guys and their mom made great sandwiches, but I didn't have much fun playing with them. Both of them, Robbie especially, were very studious and they liked to play indoors. Truthfully, I found them pretty boring.

I had a lot more fun playing with Billy Fahs. Billy and I were the same age and he liked to play outdoors, as I did. So he and I had some really good times together. Also, his folks owned the luncheonette on Mineola Boulevard so playing with Billy assured me of at least one free chocolate sundae every day.

Come to think of it, Billy and I did get into one indoor adventure. And believe me, it wasn't my fault. Here's what happened…

Billy had an air powered pellet rifle which we both enjoyed shooting. So one rainy morning, we went down into his basement, loaded up the rifle and began shooting at paper targets. Before long, we became bored with shooting at paper targets and began looking around for something more exciting to puncture or dent.

Billy found two large boxes filled with Christmas tree ornaments. He suggested, "It would be great fun to shoot at these."

I asked, "Would that be OK with your folks?"

"Yeah, sure," he said, "They won't care."

So there we were, down in the basement, shooting up two boxes of Christmas tree ornaments. About the time we destroyed the last of the ornaments, Billy's dad came down into the basement to get a wrench from his workbench. He found the two of us blasting away at the ornaments, and was clearly unhappy. Seems that Billy's assumption about it being OK to shoot at the ornaments was wrong.

His dad took the pellet rifle away from us and told us we weren't to use it again for the entire summer. And he made us pick up the six million pieces of broken ornaments. Good timing though, because about the time we finished picking up the pieces, it stopped raining. So we went outside to play. And we stayed away from Billy's folk's luncheonette that afternoon. This one day, I'd do without my chocolate sundae.

Billy and I rounded up a bunch of pennies from his house and headed over to the railroad station. We snuck by the stationhouse so the stationmaster wouldn't see us and we hopped down from the end of the platform onto the tracks where we placed our pennies. Oh yes, I should explain. Let's say you put a penny on the track and left it there for the train to run over. You know what happens? Right, the penny gets elongated by the massive weight of the train, so it's no longer round, but oval instead. Well, Billy and I did this often enough that we had quite a collection of elongated pennies.

One day, quite by accident, we discovered something most interesting and truly wonderful. We discovered that if we placed the penny about an inch off center, instead of centering it in the middle of the track, it would fire off into space just like a bullet. In fact, purely by luck, one of our one cent bullets hit a billboard off to the side of the track. The penny actually shot a hole right through the billboard. Wow! This was truly terrific! This promised to be a joyful summer for two twelve-year-old boys.

So we began placing our pennies on the track just to the right of center, thus aiming our projectiles at the billboards to the right side of the track. Now you have to understand that this "aiming" of pennies wasn't an exact science. I'd like to tell you that we got really good at shooting holes right into the middle of the billboard, but in fact, we'd be darn lucky to hit the billboard at all. But no matter, we enjoyed placing the pennies as "scientifi-cally" as we could. And we so looked forward to the next train's arrival.

But the stationmaster didn't like our playing down by the tracks. I guess he thought we might be in some sort of danger. Or maybe he figured we might do some damage. Who knows? For whatever reason, whenever he saw us playing by the tracks, he'd chase us away. So we had to be pretty sneaky when we walked by the stationhouse.

Well, on this particular day, Billy and I were down at the tracks placing an unusually large number of pennies on the track. A dozen or so, I guess. We were just finishing up our scientific placement when we heard a train whistle. A train would be coming through at high speed without stopping at the station. We started to climb back up to the platform. Oh-oh, the stationmaster, running on the platform, was coming after us. Unlike his prior chases, this time he wasn't yelling at us. Rather than trying to chase us away, he was actually trying to catch us. We had to make a run for it!

Billy and I ran beside the tracks just as fast as we could. As we ap-proached our pennies, we feared that the train might pass us there. Were that to happen, we might get shot by our own projectiles. Had the station-master not been chasing us, we would have stopped running and let the train go by, thus firing off the pennies well ahead of our arrival.

But the stationmaster was chasing us. So we ran faster, attempting to run by all of our pennies before the train caught up to us. Fortunately, we were successful. We passed by all of the pennies a few seconds before the train's arrival. But then, a frightening thought occurred to me, "What about the stationmaster? Might he get shot by our pennies?"

I turned to look back and saw that the stationmaster was no longer chasing after us. Instead, he was lying face down on the ground. Terrified, I stopped running and called to Billy, "Billy, look! The stationmaster got shot by our pennies."

Billy stopped running and turned to look back. Then he and I walked quickly toward the stationmaster to assess his condition. My heart was pounding and my stomach was churning. And my hands and knees were trembling.

Then, when we were just thirty feet from the stationmaster, he looked up at us from his prone position and scrambled to his feet. No, he hadn't been shot. He had simply fallen down while running after us.

Once again, the chase was on. Off we ran, followed by the stationmaster, angrier than ever. As he was a heavyset fellow, we easily outran him. Billy and I ran down to the next crossing, about a fourth of a mile away, turned right, and walked up the road to complete our escape.

I asked, "Hey Billy, what do you want to do now?"

He said, "Let's go climb in the big oak tree behind the post office."

"But the postmaster will come out and chase us away. Just like he did the last time," I replied.

Billy answered, "I think we can sneak by him by going through the back alley."

"Yeah, good idea. Let's go." ➤

Chapter 4

I Was a Levi's Man

WHEN I WAS A TEENAGE BOY, three brands of blue jeans were popular: Levi's, Wrangler, and Lee. Naturally, each of my friends and I could offer a convincing argument about why our particular choice was best. I was a Levi's man. Maybe it was the role that Levi's played in the history of the California gold rush, or simply the copper rivets on the pockets. I'm really not sure why. But for whatever reason, I wore Levi's.

Levi's weren't pre-shrunk. So before wearing a new pair for the first time, the wearer would first have to shrink them. And around this need to pre-shrink Levi's, all sorts of rituals arose. Somehow or another I became convinced that if I were to take a hot bath wearing my new Levi's, they'd shrink to fit my body. And so that's what I did.

I'd put on my new Levi's, plunk down into a warm bath, and just sit there. The water would soon turn sort of a dirty blue and, from the waist down, I too would turn sort of a dirty blue. After a while, the water and I would both get cold so I'd add more hot water. And I'd sit there for a while longer. I'd repeat this cycle—cool down, add hot water and sit a while longer—two or three times. All together, for maybe an hour or so.

Then I'd open the drain plug and stand up in the dirty blue water. I'd peel my way out of the Levi's, rinse myself off with a shower, and dry off with a towel. Then I'd wring out the Levi's and hang them up on the clothesline in the backyard.

Eventually, I began to suspect that maybe this ritual might be more trouble than it was worth. The novelty had worn off and I was no longer having quite so much fun sitting in warm blue water. I found myself wondering if all those gold miners out in California, back one hundred years earlier, had each spent an hour sitting in warm blue water wearing their new Levi's. Unable to envision their doing so, I began to lose interest in the ritual.

Also, I wasn't sure that the Levi's were actually shrinking to match the contours of my body. Their resultant shape seemed to be more like a pair of trousers than a person. Did my Levi's represent the shape of my lower body any more accurately than Johnny's Wranglers represented his? Unable to answer yes to this question, I modified my shrinking process. I'd take my new Levi's down into the utility room of our basement. I'd insert the rubber stopper into the concrete washbasin, toss in the Levi's, and fill the basin with hot water. I'd let the Levi's soak for maybe an hour or so, then hang them up to dry in the backyard. Kind of like any normal person would have done in the first place.

One Saturday morning—I guess I was about fourteen at the time— neither of my folks nor my brother Jerry was at home. Alone in the house, I went down to the basement utility room to shrink my new Levi's. I placed the stopper in the drain hole of the washbasin, dropped in the Levi's, and turned on the hot water. I stood there watching the water fill the basin, fully intending to turn off the tap just as soon as the basin was about half full. But within just a minute or so, the telephone rang. So I stepped from the utility room into the adjacent game room to answer the phone. Surely I could safely leave the water running while answering the phone.

The caller was my friend Mark. He asked me, "Would you like to come over to my house to play for the day?"

I said, "Sure, I'll be right over."

So I hung up the phone, walked up from the basement, and wrote a note telling my mom that I went over to Mark's house. Then I hopped on my bike and began the four-mile ride to Mark's house. Yeah, you guessed it—I forgot all about the water running in the washbasin.

Our basement had three rooms. The largest was the game room. It was pretty square, perhaps twenty feet by twenty feet. It had some furniture: a couch, a card table, and a few chairs.

One of the smaller rooms was the utility room where I was shrinking the Levi's in the washbasin. In that same room we also had the hot water heater and a workbench. This room, by the way, also served as my chemistry lab.

The other small room was a storage room. Though it was down in the basement, we used it as sort of an attic. We had any and all sorts of things in there: stuff that really didn't fit anywhere else in the house. An extra coffee table, old books, and phonograph records. Lots of clothing, family photographs, and knickknacks. I remember an old folding camera. And those super-wide ties that my dad claimed to have worn back before I was born. As we had no shelving in the storage room, and my dad could easily get cardboard boxes from his grocery store, we kept all this stuff in cardboard boxes on the floor.

OK, so there I was at Mark's house having a fine time. Then all of a sudden, I'm not sure why, I remembered the Levi's shrinking in the washbasin. And I couldn't remember if I had turned off the water. *Hmmm... did I or didn't I?* It must have been evening by then and I figured that my mom would be home. I'd simply call home and ask her to check the basement. So that's what I did.

Yes, she was home. I told her that I was still at Mark's house but that I had set the Levi's in the basin to shrink and I really couldn't remember if I'd turned off the water or not. I asked if she'd please go down into the basement to make sure that everything was OK. Yes, I'd hold the phone while she took a look.

After about one minute, Mom returned to the phone and said in an uncharacteristically stern manner, "Billy, you come right home right now!"

I asked, "Did I leave the water running? Did it overflow the basin?"

Mom didn't answer my question. She simply repeated, "Billy, you come right home right now!"

My parents didn't punish me very often, but this was one such occasion. I guess it was the nine inches of water in the basement that made them angry. Not only did I spend the next week cleaning up and drying out a terrible mess, but I was then grounded for a month. And that grounding included not being able to go down in the basement at all. This was a terrible punishment, since it meant that I wouldn't be able to experiment in my chemistry lab. And I was so looking forward to building a bomb. ➤

Chapter 5

Building Bombs

MY INTEREST IN CHEMISTRY BEGAN when I was just five years old. That's when my dad got me my first chemistry set. It was one of those Gilbert Chemistry Sets, which came in a blue metal box. It had an alcohol lamp, a test tube rack, and a bunch of small jars filled with chemicals. Some were liquid, some were powder.

Dad and I did some experiments together. I remember best our burning sulfur over the flame of the alcohol lamp. The sulfur started out as a yellow powder, then as it heated, it melted and burned with a blue flame. I thought that was pretty neat.

By the time I was twelve or so, I began doing chemistry experiments by myself. Reading chemistry books, I learned about acids and bases and about litmus paper. And I learned about how to mix two colorless liquids to produce a blue liquid. All pretty neat. I guess I was thirteen or fourteen years old when I set up a chemistry laboratory in the utility room down in the basement.

My friend Marty Jung told me about a chemical supply company in downtown New York, about an hour's trip by subway. Seemed this company would sell chemicals even to kids. The only restriction, if you were under a certain age—sixteen or eighteen, as I recall—you'd need a note from your mom or dad before they'd sell you nitric, hydrochloric or sulfuric acid. As many of the more interesting chemical reactions involve these stronger acids, I figured I'd have to pester my mom to write the required note. So that's what I did.

Once I got the note from my mom, I needed money to buy chemicals and supplies for my laboratory. I obtained the required money from three sources. First was my weekly allowance of seven dollars and fifty cents.

Second, I earned some money working in my dad's grocery store. If the decision were left to my dad, I'm sure he would have paid me a fair wage. But Uncle Dave, my dad's brother and business partner, was in charge of paying employees. And Uncle Dave consistently paid me far more than I was worth.

My third source of revenue was from gambling. Either in the basement at our house or in the basement of Arnie Davidow's house, we guys would get together to play poker. Oh, maybe two or three times a week after school. Most often I'd win. Except when Mike Hudson played in the game. Then I'd have to be real careful.

About once every couple of months, I'd come home from the chemical supply company carrying a box filled with all sorts of goodies. I was having a great time experimenting and learning about chemistry. The most important thing I learned about chemistry was that I had to do the smelly experiments when my folks weren't home. If they were to smell some of the more terrible concoctions emanating from the basement, I'd be grounded—that is, I would be barred from experimenting for some time, usually a week. And I'd be pressured into making promises to reform. So I learned to avoid such circumstances by performing the smelliest experiments when I was alone in the house.

Usually this worked out fine. Except sometimes I'd create such a long lasting terribleness (e.g. hydrogen sulfide or chlorine) that I'd be driven running from my laboratory. And the smell would still be evident some hours later when the folks arrived home. Those situations always resulted in unpleasant consequences.

One wonderful day, Marty Jung came across an old chemistry book that contained the recipe for gunpowder. "Hey, let's make some gunpowder!" we said simultaneously. Short only one ingredient and quite eager to produce gunpowder, I made a hurried trip to the chemical supply company that very week.

To be absolutely safe, Marty and I mixed up just a little bit of gunpowder on our first attempt. Out in the backyard, we poured our gunpowder onto the ground, creating a small mound about the size of a nickel. About then, we realized that we couldn't safely ignite the gunpowder with a match. We'd need a fuse. So we took about a third of our gunpowder and rolled it tightly in a piece of paper about four inches long. This resultant straw-looking invention would serve as our fuse.

We lit the fuse and moved back away as it burned toward the mound of gunpowder. "Flash!" A total success on our first try! We repeated this event two or three more times. Each time we got a bit braver, so we mixed and ignited a larger and larger mound of gunpowder.

On a number of occasions when Marty wasn't around, I'd flash gunpowder by myself, or sometimes with my brother Jerry. Often, he and I would conduct this exhibition for the entertainment of some neighborhood kids. About the thirtieth time we did so, I began to become a bit bored with the whole thing. I was ready to move on to greater challenges.

I next experimented with putting gunpowder into paper tubes to create flares and rockets. I even had two or three fireworks displays for the kids in the neighborhood. This stuff was all pretty neat, but still I was ready for even greater challenges. I began wondering how I might make gunpowder explode.

The trick to making something explode is to ignite the explosive mixture while it's in a closed container. Thus the gases created burst the container producing the explosion. But how could I ignite the gunpowder in a sealed container? That was the question. Building a firecracker seemed the obvious solution. After all, a firecracker is an enclosed paper container. And so I tried rolling firecrackers.

That didn't work so well. I think my problem was that I never did perfect the fuse. Each time, my fuse would go out at the entry to the firecracker. I'd have to come up with another scheme. It was then that my brother Jerry suggested we use a magnesium fuse. Though he was only about nine or ten at the time, he remembered my having demonstrated that magnesium is highly flammable.

We both knew that if a strip of magnesium were to become very hot, it would burn very quickly—with a flash. Certainly the flash of burning magnesium would ignite the gunpowder. But how could I heat the magnesium strip in a closed container filled with gunpowder? Ah yes, of course! Electricity. All I had to do was to fill a jar with gunpowder, then carefully insert a fuse consisting of a magnesium strip stretched between two wires—just like the filament in an incandescent light bulb. I could then use 115 volt electricity from the wall socket to ignite my bomb. And that's what I did.

The first bomb I made was really very small. It consisted of a small paper tube wrapped in electrical tape. My fuse was simply a magnesium strip attached to a long electrical wire. I placed bomb number one in the concrete washbasin down in the basement utility room. Then I inserted the plug end of the electrical wire into the wall socket. Bam! It worked! Success on my first try. I was elated.

I made a few more bombs all larger than the first. And almost every time, the bomb exploded just fine. I got to make such a loud bang that I actually scared myself—even though I was the fellow igniting the bomb. And that gave me a terrific idea. What if I were to surprise somebody else? What if I were to set a bomb in the washbasin and let somebody else unknowingly ignite it? I figured that would really be terrific.

The light in the utility room was simply a bare bulb screwed into a socket in the middle of the ceiling. Convenient to my plan, the light switch was an old-fashioned pull chain. That was perfect! I could wire my fuse to an electrical plug and replace the light bulb with a screw-in, electrical socket. Once coupling the plug and socket, I'd invite someone to turn on the light and "Bam!" That would be great! But whom?

Fred, that's whom.

My friend Fred Gifford was a good-natured fellow who was just as curious about chemistry as I. Fred would gladly step into the utility room to look in on the latest experiment on the laboratory workbench. And once in the utility room, he'd, naturally, pull the chain to turn on the light.

So one day after school, three or four of the guys were playing poker down in the basement's game room. I think that Arnie Davidow was there, and Marty Goldman, my brother Jerry, and I can't remember who else. We were waiting for Fred.

Fred knew we'd be playing poker that day, and I figured he might come by to join in the game. To encourage his visit, I had invited him over to see my latest experiment.

And he came. Down to the basement and over to the poker table. Fred asked about the experiment which I earlier mentioned. So I said something like, "It's over there in the laboratory. Go in there and turn on the light and take a look."

Fred stepped into the utility room, reached for the chain to turn on the light, and pulled it firmly.

Oh yes, I need to tell you how I set up the bomb. I didn't want to hurt Fred. I just wanted to surprise him. So I was sure to wrap the bomb with lots of electrical tape. I placed the bomb in the concrete washbasin and covered it with a bunch of wadded up newspaper. Then, per Jerry's suggestion, I placed a piece of plywood over the whole lot of newspaper. Both Jerry and I figured that the exploding gasses might push the plywood up just a few inches. We thought, surely the plywood would remain in the washbasin. But that isn't exactly what happened.

When Fred pulled the chain, intending to turn on the light, everything worked just fine. That is, the fuse worked and the bomb exploded. Man, did it explode! In fact, in all of my experiments, I'd never heard such an explosion. For us in the next room, it was frightening. What it must have been like for Fred in the laboratory, we'd soon find out.

First of all, the sound of the explosion made him leap off to the side away from the washbasin. So he ended up lying on the floor, leaning up against the far wall. And the plywood, which I figured would hop up just a few inches? Well, I was wrong. The plywood flew up to the ceiling and down on poor Fred. And all of that wadded up old newspaper? Well, it all went up in flames. For the life of me, I couldn't figure out how that could happen.

Anyway, the next thing we knew, the poker game was over. The whole poker playing crowd ran into the laboratory. There we found Fred lying on the floor, leaning against the far wall, holding his hands over his chest, and gasping for breath. We figured that maybe he had stopped breathing for a time.

Not only that, but all of the burning newspaper was now all about the room. So there we were, a bunch of former poker players, using water from the washbasin to extinguish flames about the laboratory.

From that day on, Fred was most careful to look before turning on the light in the utility room. ➤

Chapter 6

The Portable Bomb

BY TRIAL AND ERROR MAINLY, I expanded my knowledge of pyrotechnics. In addition to advancing my skill with gunpowder, I got pretty good with various kinds of flash powder. So I could make fireworks and flares and bombs that not only exploded but exploded with a flash of color and with flaming sparks all over the place. All pretty neat.

The thing I was most eager to develop was a portable bomb. As long as I was using the 115-volt electricity from the wall or the light socket, I was limited to explosions within an extension cord's length of the house. But I yearned to take my bombs far and wide. So I worked on refining my magnesium fuse so I could ignite it with dry cell batteries—just like they do with dynamite. I figured if 115 volts could flash a wide magnesium ribbon, then dry cell batteries ought to flash a narrow magnesium ribbon. It was all a matter of working out the geometry.

After some fooling with shaving down a wide magnesium ribbon to the proper size, I began to experience some success. Experimenting with the fuse only—no bomb—I was able to flash a narrow magnesium ribbon using the energy from two dry cell batteries. No, it wasn't as reliable as a wider ribbon with 115 volts, but I did manage to flash the narrow ribbon using two dry cells about once every two tries. Good enough! It was now time to try this system on a real bomb. A small one, of course.

I figured that since I was building a portable bomb, I should go outside to ignite it. So I went out to the backyard. I was concerned that the neighbors might be alarmed if I were to make a loud noise, so I buried the bomb about twelve inches in the ground. Then by jumping up and down on it, I packed soil back into the hole. I ran my electrical wires about thirty feet back into the garage. I sat there with my two dry cell batteries, electrical wire in hand.

Now here's what I figured would happen: I thought that since the bomb was as small as it was, and the hole was as deep as it was, and the soil packed down as well as it was, the bomb would simply puff up the soil a bit. Like maybe the soil would mound up so that it would look like an anthill. And perhaps the bomb wouldn't even explode. After all, my fuses were working only about 50 percent of the time.

So in the garage, electrical wires in hand, I ducked behind some boxes, just in case. Then I touched the wires to the terminals of the dry cell batteries. And for about a second, nothing happened. Then, just as I began thinking that my fuse was a dud, I heard sort of an explosion. I say *sort of* an explosion because it wasn't like any of the explosions I had made down in the utility room. This sound was entirely different. More like a *whoosh* than a *bam*. I figured that's because the bomb was buried in the ground and because I was outdoors where the sound wouldn't echo as it would indoors.

In any event, I heard this *whoosh*, and I saw what looked like a bunch of soil flying straight up in the air. As I was well back in the garage, I couldn't look up in the air, but only straight ahead. So I could see only about eight or ten feet of airspace above the ground. But that entire eight- or ten-foot space was filled with stuff moving straight up. Then, a few seconds later, I heard a bunch of stuff, like maybe soil and rocks, landing somewhere nearby.

I walked slowly out of the garage, on the one hand excited by my success, but on the other hand surprised by what I saw. My bomb had blown quite a significant hole in the ground. But where in the world did all that soil go? It wasn't too long before I found out.

What sounded like a *whoosh* to me was apparently somewhat more. In fact, there must have been some *bam* along with the *whoosh*. Within seconds, neighbors appeared from all around. And now I need to tell you about Mr. and Mrs. Hoff.

Mr. And Mrs. Hoff lived next door. And Mr. Hoff had this beautiful, brand-new, royal blue Cadillac. That car was his pride and joy. And on that day when I blew the hole in the ground, Mr. Hoff's Cadillac was parked out behind his house, just over the fence from our backyard. Yes, I know I should have noticed it earlier, but his Cadillac being in the backyard was a rare occurrence, because he almost always parked it in the garage. And besides, who knew that the bomb would do any more than mound up a little dirt? After all, this was an experiment.

And on that particular day, Mrs. Hoff had a bunch of newly washed laundry hanging on the clothesline. So there they were—the Cadillac and the wet clothes in the backyard. Well, remember all the soil missing from the hole? And how I was wondering where all that soil had gone? And remember the sound I heard of the soil and the rocks falling? Well, for some strange reason, all of the soil went over the fence to Mr. And Mrs. Hoff's yard and much of it landed on Mr. Hoff's Cadillac and on Mrs. Hoff's wash.

Mrs. Hoff had to wash all of her clothes over again. Woefully, I spent the rest of that day washing Mr. Hoff's Cadillac. Then I spent the next day waxing Mr. Hoff's Cadillac. And I was grounded. I wasn't allowed to do any chemistry experiments, bombs or otherwise, for a very long time.

The Battery

I learned in Mr. Stern's science class that a person's tongue is extremely sensitive to electrical energy. This bit of information, I figured, would enable me to play another trick on Fred.

A few days later, he and I were doing our homework upstairs in my bedroom. Before too long, I innocently asked Fred, "Do you know how to tell if a battery still has some remaining energy?" Fred said he didn't know so I told him, "You simply taste the terminals. Yeah, you place your tongue between both terminals at the same time, and if they taste salty, the battery is out of energy, or almost out of energy." After a bit more conversation, I volunteered to find a battery if Fred would like to try the experiment. He said, "Sure," so I went downstairs to find a battery.

Now I have to tell you about the battery I brought back upstairs. Today, in the twenty-first century, all of the batteries we use in our radios and other personal electronics devices are pretty low voltage—generally 1-1/2 volts. That's because all of our modern electronics devices are made with semiconductors, which require low voltage. Well, this incident of Fred tasting the battery happened about 1957 or so. And in those days, we didn't have low voltage semiconductor devices. Instead we had vacuum tubes. And vacuum tubes operated not on low voltage, but on high voltage.

So when I came back upstairs with a battery for Fred to taste, it wasn't a 1-1/2 volt battery. Instead it was an 85 volt battery. The darn thing was about eight inches long and weighed maybe two pounds. Conveniently, the battery had both of its terminals right up there on top about one-half inch apart. Perfect for Fred to taste with one lick. So I gave the battery to Fred and he pulled it up to his mouth, stuck out his tongue, and licked it.

Well I knew Fred would have some sort of reaction. But I had no idea he'd react so instantly or so violently! First of all, the sound he made was remarkable. It was kind of a groan and a grunt at the same time. And his groan-grunt was followed by the sound of air rushing out of his lungs. He lurched backward in his chair and his eyes opened really wide.

But the worst part was what he did with the battery. Seemingly in the same instant as he was doing the grunt-groan, air-from-the-lungs thing, he snapped his arm out in front of him flinging the battery across the room in my direction. No, I don't think that Fred intentionally threw the battery at me. Why would he? Nonetheless, I found myself ducking and at the same time listening to the battery crashing into the lamp on my desk, then into the wall behind the desk. One broken lamp, one significant dent in the wall. Fred was speechless for some minutes. All in all, a pretty exciting experiment.

From that day on, gullible as Fred was, he remained extremely cautious about anything I said or asked him to do. ➤

Chapter 7

The Mona Lisa

AS YOU KNOW, **LEONARDO DA VINCI'S MONA LISA** remains on display in the Louvre in Paris, France. But every once in a while, this most famous painting goes on tour to the major museums of the world. One such tour occurred in the early 1960s.

I was attending college in New York when the Mona Lisa displayed at the city's Metropolitan Museum of Art. One Friday evening, two class-mates and I were on our way to a dance at a nurses' college, also in New York. Marvin was driving his old Studebaker. I sat in the front right seat, and Henry, a tall skinny fellow, draped himself across the back seat.

Our driving route took us past the Metropolitan Museum of Art where we noticed people walking up the steps toward the museum's entrance. Marvin expressed surprise that the museum was open during the evening. But recalling a newspaper article about the Mona Lisa's visit, I said, "Maybe the museum has extended its visitor hours." Then I suggested, "Hey guys, since we're right here, let's stop to see the Mona Lisa."

Marvin and Henry weren't enthusiastic about my suggestion. I think they were more interested in getting to the dance. Marvin said something about us not being able to find a place to park. But just then, a car pulled away from a parking place directly across from the museum. I shouted, "Park right there! Park right there!"

Somewhat reluctantly, Marvin parked the car.

As we walked up the steps to the entrance, we noticed that everyone else was dressed really fancy. Men in tuxedos, ladies in long gowns, furs and jewelry. So we figured that maybe this was some kind of a special crowd. But heck, we were already there. And besides, we were dressed nicely. Henry was wearing his plaid jacket. Marvin wore his new green sweater. And both Marvin and I were wearing leather shoes. We'd be OK.

At the top of the steps, just in front of the entry door, a woman in a long, navy blue evening gown asked to see our invitation.

"Invitation?" I responded.

She explained that the evening's event was a pre-opening party. And that only members of the museum, plus invitees of Mayor Robert Wagner were attending. She was polite, but she turned us away.

Walking down the steps, Henry said something about leaving to go to the dance. But I insisted that we were going to see the Mona Lisa. I wasn't sure how we'd get inside, but I figured that the museum would certainly have a freight entrance. Or maybe an open window. So I told the guys, "Follow me."

We went around to the side of the museum, and sure enough we found the freight entrance. The door was open. And no one else was around.

Inside, just to the right of the door, was the freight elevator. We pushed the elevator's call button and waited. A few seconds later, the elevator arrived and the door opened. "Oh-oh," there stood an elevator operator. A big burly fellow with a grey beard opened the elevator's cage door. Somewhat nervously, we stepped inside.

The elevator operator asked, "Where to boys?"

"Back upstairs to the Mona Lisa," I replied.

He peered at me and asked, "Have you been up there already?"

I said, "Yes, we just came down to put a dime in the parking meter."

Then he turned to face me directly, looked me straight in the eye and asked, "You're lying to me, aren't you kid?"

Nervously, I answered, "Yes sir, I am, but we'd sure like to see the Mona Lisa. Would you take us up there please?"

Just a slight pause, then a broad grin as he closed the elevator door and announced, "Mona Lisa, coming right up."

In unison, Marvin, Henry, and I said, "Thank you."

The elevator operator instructed, "Turn right as you exit the elevator and just walk in there like you own the place." I assured him we'd do that just fine. And we did.

Three minutes later, Marvin, Henry, and I were standing smack dab in front of the most famous painting in the world. I had heard that Mona Lisa's smile was hypnotic. So I studied her mouth carefully. *Yes, her smile is sort of hypnotic,* I thought. *I wonder if ...*

Henry interrupted my thought with, "Hey, where is everybody?"

I looked around and realized that we were nearly alone with the Mona Lisa. Most everyone else was on the other side of the room socializing with the mayor and enjoying champagne and hors d'oeuvres.

"Hey guys, look, champagne and hors d'oeuvres," I suggested.

But both Marvin and Henry insisted it was time to leave. Marvin started back toward the freight elevator, but I said, "No, let's go out through the front entrance. I'd like to say 'good evening' to the lady who earlier turned us away."

As we walked out through the front entry door, we all wished her a very nice evening. Poor dear, we left her speechless.

I think this story offers three valuable lessons. First, and most obvious, persistence pays. That's clear.

Second, if you're in a freight elevator, and the elevator operator catches you lying to him, come right back at him with the absolute truth and a direct request for help.

And third, whenever you're in New York and you're on your way to a dance at a nurses' college—so you're all dressed up anyway—be on the lookout for cultural opportunities. ➤

Chapter 8

The Hitchhiker in the Dark

OON AFTER OBTAINING MY DRIVER'S LICENSE, I began picking up hitchhikers. Whenever asked about this new habit of mine, I explained that I simply want to help my fellow man. But the truth was that I was just plain curious about the people who stood on the side of the road with their thumb stuck out. I figured it would be interesting to talk with them and find out what they were all about.

Picking up hitchhikers led to some really interesting adventures. Like the time I drove up to Cortland, New York. I was in college at the time and I'd been dating a girl who attended the teachers' school at Cortland State. She had invited me up to the campus for homecoming weekend.

My friend Myron Feinstein, who had also been dating a girl from Cortland, told me that he could drive up there in as little as five hours. So there I was one Thursday evening in October, speeding my way thru central New York farm country trying to beat Myron's five-hour record.

About ten o'clock or so, out there in the midst of the farm fields, I saw a fellow standing in the pitch black with his thumb stuck out. He wore a light, black jacket and carried a medium-sized paper sack. I guess the guy was in his thirties, six-foot tall and medium build.

I stopped the car. He opened the door and sat down in the front passenger seat. Then I asked him, "How come you're hitchhiking out in the country this time of night?"

He said, "Oh, I had some car trouble and had to abandon my car. I have a friend in Cortland so that's where I'm going."

I told him, "You're in luck because that's where I'm going too."

He didn't tell me much more about himself. Instead, he asked a lot of questions. He seemed curious about where I was going. Why I was driving through New York farm country in the middle of the night. Where I was staying in Cortland. And how long I would be there.

About an hour and a half later we arrived in Cortland. I asked him, "Would you like me to drive you to your friend's house?"

He said, "I'll just get out at the motel where you're staying."

I pulled up in front of the motel. He stepped out and said, "Thanks for the ride."

I watched him disappear into the darkness as he walked down the road. It was close to midnight.

I got pretty busy over the weekend—football, drinking beer, partying. You know, typical college homecoming stuff. So I hardly even thought about the hitchhiker.

Returning to the motel on Saturday afternoon, I found a note on the door to my room. The note was from the motel manager, and it said that I'd had a call from Captain Clark of the New York State Troopers, the state police force. The captain wanted me to call him at his office right away.

Oh hell. I figured some state trooper saw me speeding through the farm country on Thursday night, trying to beat Myron's record time. And now I'd probably get a speeding ticket.

So I called the captain. His first question was, "Did you pick up a hitchhiker on your drive up to Cortland last Thursday night?"

I said, "Yes, I did."

My yes answer led to a long series of questions. The captain wanted to know where I picked him up. And if he were alone. And what he was wearing. And what he was carrying with him. And what he and I talked about. And if he'd given me any information regarding where he was and what he was doing before I picked him up.

Following his questions about the hitchhiker, the captain also asked me for my address and phone number so he might get in touch with me if he later had further questions.

When it seemed that he was finished asking questions, I put one to him. I said, "Captain, I know I broke the law. I know it's illegal to pick up a hitchhiker in the State of New York. And I shouldn't have stopped. But the questions you're asking me suggest you're investigating a crime far more significant than hitchhiking. Could you tell me what's so special about this fellow I picked up last Thursday night?"

The captain replied, "Yes, Mr. Birnbaum, I can. The man you picked up last Thursday night is a professional hijacker. An hour or so before you picked him up, he knocked out a truck driver over in the farm country. Then he stole the driver's wallet and ransacked the truck. Your picking him up served as an important part of his getaway."

I think I said thank you to the captain before I hung up the phone. But I'm really not sure. I staggered for a few steps and it took me a while to regain my composure. Then I realized that I'd have a heck of a good story to tell my grandchildren. And if I were to refrain from picking up hitch-hikers, then maybe someday I'd actually have some grandchildren. ➤

Part Two

A Young Man in California

MY TIMING WAS EXCELLENT. I graduated from college with a degree in electrical engineering at the height of both the space program and the defense build-up. So, for sure, I would earn a decent salary and have my choice among a number of employment opportunities.

The job offer in Boston was actually the most interesting. But I really wanted to move to California. I had heard such wonderful things about the Golden State. You know, like free love and nickel beer. (Not true though—I never paid less than twenty-five cents for a beer.)

And from all those 1950s cowboy movies I'd seen, I knew that a guy could ride his horse out from Los Angeles and, in twenty minutes, he'd be setting up camp in the shade of a mesquite tree beside a babbling brook.

Hal and Irwin, two college classmates of mine, and I left New York on the morning of February 2, headed for California. It was nineteen degrees and there was snow on the ground.

Each of us had one suitcase containing clothing, toiletries, and a freshly printed diploma.

This was it! After all those years of talking about moving out west, I was actually doing it. I remember looking down at the Hudson River as we drove across the George Washington Bridge. I think those were butterflies in my stomach.

Irwin's old Nash Rambler made the cross-country trip with no major problems. Though we did have to stop every fifty miles or so to pour in another can of motor oil. And since gasoline was then only twenty-three cents per gallon, motor oil was our higher expense.

When we arrived in southern California on the afternoon of February 9, it was seventy-eight degrees and the surfers were driving home from the beach. I unpacked my suitcase and stayed for the next four decades.

And, while living in southern California, I had my share of interesting adventures.

Chapter 9

Travels

MY ROOMMATE, GARY, HAD LOANED US his Jeep panel wagon. I was driving the first shift and my friend Ben was sitting to my right. Our destination was northern Arizona where we had planned to hunt mountain lion. As I had previously hunted only small game—jack rabbits mostly—this would be my first hunt for larger game. I was both excited and nervous.

As we approached the on-ramp to the Riverside Freeway, a hitchhiker was thumbing a ride. He was a medium-sized guy carrying a small suitcase. As I stopped to let him in, Ben gave me a particularly unpleasant glance. That was my reminder that Ben didn't approve of picking up hitchhikers. Following his unpleasant glance, Ben hopped over the seatback declaring, "I'll ride in the back." The panel wagon didn't have a back seat, just a flat-bed covered with a foam mattress. So as the hitchhiker hopped aboard, Ben made himself comfortable amongst a bunch of camping gear, rifles, and ammunition.

Then the usual dialog between driver and hitchhiker: "Where are you going?" "How come you're hitchhiking?" Stuff like that. But the dialog remained two-way only. Ben wanted no part of the conversation. He was lying in the back with his eyes closed. Falling asleep, I supposed.

The hitchhiker told me, "I'm going back to Texas. That's where I came from yesterday."

I waited a long time before asking him, "Gee, one day isn't very long to spend here in California. How come your visit was so short?"

"Oh, I just had to visit my wife. Straighten a few things out."

I was certainly curious. *Hmm, I thought. He's returning to Texas like that's where he's from. But his wife's here. And he visited her for just one day. And what did he mean, straighten a few things out?* I looked over to the back of the Jeep and noticed that Ben's eyes were closed. *Good, he's asleep.*

I waited a very long time before asking my next question, "What are you going to do when you get back to Texas?"

He thought for a while and replied, "Oh, I'm going to turn myself in to the sheriff." I glanced in the back and saw that Ben was asleep. *Good, I thought. I don't want him to hear any of this. Certainly he'd give me an especially hard time about picking up this fellow.*

I was almost afraid to ask the next question, but my curiosity was killing me. "Turn yourself in to the sheriff? For what?"

After a brief pause, he replied, "Breaking and entering, assault and battery, and attempted murder."

Again I hesitated, but I just had to ask the next question. "Gee, did you do any of those things?"

He thought for quite a while. Like he was actually trying to figure it out for himself. Finally he answered, "No, not really."

I glanced over my shoulder into the back of the Jeep. Ben was still asleep. But now I was starting to worry. *Might this guy be dangerous? Maybe he's armed.*

Ben was back there sleeping amongst our unloaded firearms. And I was unarmed. For the first time, it occurred to me that it might be better if Ben were awake. But then I reconsidered, *Ah hell. What am I worrying about? It's broad daylight. I'm simply giving the guy a ride. No big deal.*

Unable to leave good enough alone, I asked, "Are you sure the sheriff's after you on those charges?"

"Yeah, he is. He arrested me once, but I escaped."

Not too much more conversation after that. I mean, what more do you ask a guy who had to think for a while before saying that he's not really guilty of breaking and entering, assault and battery, and attempted murder? And then he breaks out of jail. But then he's going back to surrender. I was out of questions. So we drove along, the hitchhiker and I riding silently and Ben sleeping in the back.

About twenty minutes later, we arrived at the highway junction in Riverside. Ben and I would continue northeast through Barstow, while our hitchhiker would travel east thru Phoenix. So we dropped him off at the junction. He stepped out of the car, said, "Thanks for the ride," and closed the door behind him.

I drove away thinking, *Good thing Ben slept through that conversation. If he had heard it, he'd give me a hard time for sure.*

Just then, Ben hopped over from the back, plopped down in the front seat with his arms folded, and with an all-knowing look about him said, "So your buddy's a jailbird, huh?"

Independence Hall

I was twenty-six years old, that rainy Tuesday morning in October, when I visited Independence Hall. As I entered the historic building, I saw very few people. Apparently, not many would-be historians were willing to brave the morning rain. A park ranger—Independence Hall is a National Historical Park—was lecturing to a small group near the Liberty Bell. A man and a woman were browsing in the museum. I hurried by both of these locations, having a specific destination in mind. I wanted to visit the meeting room where our forefathers had signed the Declaration of Independence.

Entering the signing room, I noticed that the rear third of the room served as a visitors' gallery. It had perhaps three or four rows of seats. A three-foot high, white wood rail separated the visitors from the front, the business end, of the room. Kind of like a courtroom. The front two-thirds of the room, on the other side of the rail, was probably very much like it was back in 1776. There were twenty or so small desks with a chair at each. And two fireplaces, one at either side of the room.

To my surprise, I was the only visitor in the room. Off to the left side of the room, down in front, was a park ranger. A young lady, perhaps in her mid-twenties. She wore the traditional brown uniform and wide-brimmed Smokey-the-Bear hat. She said, "Good morning."

"Good morning," I replied.

She asked me if I had any specific questions.

"Yes, I have. What are those little compartments in the wall next to the fireplaces?"

"Those compartments were for the gentlemen to place their gloves into to dry them out and keep them warm."

"Oh, I see. Thank you." I strolled around a bit, on my side of the rail. All the while looking around at the desks, the walls, the fireplace, and the various objects in the room. I was taken in by a sense of history. I recall thinking, *I'm standing in the very same room where our forefathers signed the Declaration of Independence.*

And then I asked the ranger, "Do you know which of the signers of the Declaration used which desks? For example, do you know which of these desks was used by Benjamin Franklin?"

She moved toward a desk near the rail, "Yes, this is the desk where

Benjamin Franklin sat." Pointing toward another nearby desk, she said, "This desk is where Samuel Adams sat. Our historians know which desks were used by about two-thirds of the signers of the Declaration, but they're unsure of the remaining third."

Then I asked, "About the artifacts on the desks—the cups, ash trays, spectacles, and books, for example—were they actually owned by the individuals who used the desks? Or are they simply of the period and placed by the park service for effect?"

She began walking toward me as she answered, "Some are simply of the period and recently added for effect." She pointed to an example or two. A book on one desk, a pair of gloves on another. Continuing to walk toward me, she added, "Others are known to have been owned by specific signers of the Declaration." She pointed to a book on Benjamin Franklin's desk and told me, "This book, for example, is Benjamin Franklin's. We know from the notes he wrote in the margins on some of the pages."

She took another step toward me as she reached for a walking cane on another desk. As she moved close to me, she used both hands to hold the cane out horizontally in front of her. She seemed to be handing the cane to me across the wood rail. I held up my hands to receive the cane. About the time the cane passed from her hands to mine, she said, "And this is Thomas Jefferson's cane."

A long silence followed. I held the cane in both my hands. I stood motionless. My eyes grew wet. So the cane, and the ranger, and the entire room became a blur.

She explained, "In those days, it was customary for a gentleman to present a cane to his best friend."

She showed me the inscription on the cane's silver handle. I looked and I saw, though blurry. But still, I couldn't speak. I don't know how long I stood there frozen and glassy-eyed. Sooner or later, I handed the cane back to the ranger, thanked her, and left Independence Hall.

I stepped out into the soft rain and slowly walked some twenty or thirty yards. Then I turned for my last look at Independence Hall. I stood there gazing, for two or three minutes perhaps.

I felt a strange sensation in my hands—as if I were still holding Thomas Jefferson's cane. Looking down at my hands, I felt raindrops sliding down my cheeks.

Or maybe they were tears.

Saint Cloud

In the late 1960s, my partner, Dorian, and I developed monitoring equipment used by electric utility companies. We sold our products through a network of independent sales agents throughout the United States. In August of 1969, I traveled to Minneapolis, Minnesota, to make a series of sales calls with our mid-west sales agent based in that city. Since the sales agent owned a private plane—a four-seat, single-engine Mooney—we decided to fly, rather than drive, to our scheduled sales meeting in Saint Cloud, Minnesota, some seventy miles away.

At a small airport just outside of Minneapolis, we rolled the plane from its hanger. As our pilot, Bob sat front left. As co-pilot, Don sat front right. I climbed into the back seat behind Don and carefully placed my demonstration instrument—a transformer fault detector—on the seat to my left.

"Prop clear," Bob shouted, as he started up the engine. He taxied the plane out to the runway. Then *vroom,* we were on our way. We climbed to about twenty-five hundred feet. Pretty day. Bright blue sky. Small white puffy clouds. I enjoyed looking down at the farmland below.

We flew east toward Saint Paul and were nearing that city when, all of a sudden, the engine began to sputter. Bob quickly reached for the throttle. Don began scrambling, seemingly reaching for *everything*. Then all became quiet. The engine had stopped.

Bob tried frantically to restart the engine. No luck. We were quickly losing altitude. I looked down and saw green fields dotted with cows grazing peacefully. I figured Bob would simply put us down, quite gently, in one of those soft, green pastures. Bob's biggest challenge, I supposed, would be to avoid hitting a cow. But while I was looking for the least cow-populated pasture, Bob kept flying, or falling, toward downtown Saint Paul. Our view changed from soft, green fields to houses, then to mid-rise buildings.

Bob and Don both knew something I didn't: Saint Paul had a downtown airport. So while I was trying to decide upon my favorite soft, green field, Don was calling to arrange an emergency landing. The control tower told us that we could land wherever we liked. The runway if we could make it; the taxiway was fine too. Even the far side of the parking lot, over by a fence.

Looking out through the front window, I soon spotted the airport. Down, down we dropped. We hit the runway pretty hard. I thought the landing gear might collapse but it stayed intact. We bounced hard a few times and then began to roll. To my right, hiding between two hangars, were a fire truck and an ambulance. As we rolled by, both vehicles came following behind, their emergency lights flashing. Like maybe they expected our plane might catch fire. But it didn't catch fire. It just rolled to a stop near the terminal building.

The four-seat Mooney had just one door—on the right. So Don had to exit first. Bob turned to Don and instructed, "OK, Don, let's get out."

But Don didn't move. And he didn't speak. "Hey Don, let's get out," Bob repeated.

Still, Don didn't move and didn't speak. Two firemen ran up to the plane shouting at Don to get out. But still, he didn't move or speak. One of the firemen then opened the door, grabbed Don by the collar, and pulled him out of the plane. Next Bob, and then I, scurried out.

The firemen carried Don off the plane and into the terminal building. They plopped him down on a chair in the coffee shop. He sat there for twenty minutes or so before he could speak. And almost an hour before he could walk. With help. Seems that he became so frightened that he went into shock.

After about an hour, Bob's wife arrived to drive us back to Minneapolis. No, we never did get to our meeting in Saint Cloud that day. Come to think of it, I've never been to Saint Cloud.

The Ansel Adams Museum

Throughout the 1990s, I was quite active as an amateur photographer. Generally, I used black and white film and, often, I photographed landscapes. It was no surprise then, that I much admired the work of the renowned landscape photographer, Ansel Adams. Adams was born in 1902 and passed away in 1984. Appropriately, the Ansel Adams Museum is located in San Francisco, the city in which he grew up.

During the 1990s, I often traveled to San Francisco for business, so I occasionally visited the museum. On one particular occasion, about 1996, I checked into the San Francisco Marriott Hotel and, as was my custom, I walked up to the concierge desk to ask about that week's exhibits in the Ansel Adams Museum. As I approached the desk, I noted a new face. Though I had stayed in the Marriott many times, I hadn't before seen this particular young lady. I figured she was new.

I asked if she could tell me what was on display at the Ansel Adams Museum.

She replied, "He's not always there."

Not wishing to be impolite, I didn't tell her that, were she referring to Ansel Adams, he'd been dead for over a decade. I simply repeated her statement as a question, "He's not always there?"

"No, he travels a lot," she replied.

"Oh, he travels a lot?" By now, she and I had established a sort of a rhythm to our conversation. Clearly, I was the straight man.

"Yes, he travels a lot. And when he does, he takes much of his work with him."

I found that last comment particularly interesting. It conjured up, for me, the vision of a dead photographer, standing behind a large view camera mounted on a sturdy wooden tripod—all the while holding a dozen or so framed photographs under each arm.

Before I could reply "Oh he takes much of his work with him?" She added, "But the museum often displays the work of other photographers."

Ah, finally! Now I might actually get some useful information! I asked her, "Do you know which other photographers have their work on display at the museum this week?"

She reached for a copy of *What's Happening in San Francisco* and began thumbing through the pages. Within a minute or so I had my answer. I thanked her and departed.

Two evenings later, I visited the Ansel Adams Museum. And, as it turned out, the young concierge was correct—some other photographers had their work on display. I looked around for him, but Ansel Adams wasn't there that evening. He must have been traveling. And only a few of his photographs were there on display. I suppose he took much of his work with him. ➤

Chapter 10

Mount Sill

MOUNT SILL IS LOCATED in the Palisades region of California's Sierra Nevada range. In the summer of 1977, we attempted to climb that majestic peak. And we might have been successful, if only we'd taken the more direct route. That first chute on the right.

We were a party of fifteen. Eddie led the climb and I was the assistant leader. Though this was an official Sierra Club outing, it was different from the trips that Eddie and I had led together in the past, as neither Eddie nor I had previously climbed Mount Sill. It's customary, and a darn good idea, for both the leader and the assistant leader to do the climb first, before leading it as a club-sponsored outing. This would be one of those occasional "exploratory" trips. Oh sure, we had spoken with others who had climbed the mountain. And we'd read the route descriptions in the climber's guide. But we had no firsthand experience on Mount Sill.

We carefully selected the members of our party. Jack Cole, Dave Franzen, Jeff Ross—each an experienced climber in top condition.

At a moderate pace, we hiked up the eight or so miles to a base camp above Sam Mack Meadow. There, on a broad shelf, just under the saddle between Mount Galey and Mount Sill, at an elevation of about 12,500 feet, we made camp for the night. We had gained about 5,000 feet for the day—a healthy climb with full packs. We were all pretty tired, so we simply relaxed in camp that evening. As the sun was setting, we enjoyed a magnificent view of the long granite slab descending some 1,500 feet back down to Third Lake. And we marveled at the beautiful red afterglow on the surrounding granite peaks.

With our camp tucked up against Mount Sill, we didn't have a view of the summit. But we could see the massive rock wall at the base of the saddle. With the summit at 14,200 feet, and our camp at 12,500, we'd have only 1,700 feet to climb the next day. But it was a tough 1,700 feet. First, we'd gain about 500 feet climbing the rock wall to the top of the saddle between Mount Galey and Mount Sill. Then across the glacier for a distance, which Eddie and I hotly debated. Then up one chute or another—which specific chute we also debated. And then a scramble to the top.

Eddie and I agreed on about half of our route—up the wall to the saddle and onto the glacier. But as to which chute to enter and climb, that's where we differed. And we differed strongly. Eddie had read about a more challenging "alternative route," which he was eager to try. I figured that, since this was an exploratory trip, we should stick with the more traditional route. He couldn't convince me and I couldn't convince him. But he was the leader, and I the assistant. And he said we were going up the fourth chute, so that's the way we'd go.

We awoke just before daylight, gobbled down a cold breakfast, packed up and started hiking. I knew that climbing the rock wall would be challenging. From camp, I could see that it was nearly vertical. But the rock was irregular enough that it did offer good hand and footholds.

We were able to climb the wall without using a rope. But the climb up was tough enough that it was slow. I worried a bit about our climb down that afternoon, because the wall would make for a difficult, and potentially dangerous, descent. To mentally prepare for our eventual climb down, I looked back behind me to "mark" the route we'd later descend.

What a magnificent view from the saddle! Mount Galey rose up on our left, and the glacier lay before us. And off to our right—so close we could almost touch it—that magnificent hunk of dark granite, Mount Sill. As we walked up to the glacier, the first chute came clearly into view. It seemed logical that we should climb that chute. So as we strapped our crampons onto our boots, and we lathered up with sunscreen, I once again tried to convince Eddie. But he wasn't about to be swayed. And as we walked along the glacier—on the way to the fourth chute—I could see what I believed to be the correct route, disappearing behind us.

To arrive at the fourth chute, we'd be traveling a fourth of a mile or so along the glacier. As it was then late morning, the sun's reflection off the snow made us extremely hot. And the altitude was high enough that traveling along the glacier was fatiguing. We stopped frequently to rest. I guess it took us about an hour to travel the fourth of a mile. And finally, there it was—the fourth chute. Gee, it was steep. And narrow. And, oh-oh, below the chute were a number of large boulders—a sign of recent rock fall.

Again I spoke to Eddie. Not so much trying to talk him into the route I thought was correct. Instead, I tried to talk him out of a route I then feared dangerous. But Eddie figured that the fourth chute would take us to the top of the mountain. And, come hell or high water, that's the way we were going.

Three or four of the more aggressive climbers were eager to follow. Hey, steepness, loose rock, maybe a route to the summit. Maybe not. Well, maybe that's the kind of excitement *they* were hoping for when they got into this sport.

But others were apprehensive. They'd be pleased to let a smaller party enter the chute and attempt to reach the top. They'd be perfectly happy to follow along later.

So into the chute went Eddie, followed by three of the more aggressive climbers. Then followed by me. The chute was narrow and irregularly shaped, so I couldn't see the climbers ahead. I did hear an occasional voice communication. A shout here, a reply there.

But the shouts and replies didn't bring good news. The four climbers ahead of me were grunting and swearing. Two of them shouted up to Eddie, asking questions about the route. Eddie's hesitant answers were discouraging. I interpreted his long periods of silence as an indication that the route didn't "go." That we were working very hard to arrive at a dead end.

And I was seriously concerned about taking a party of fifteen climbers into a steep chute filled with loose boulders. If a rock were kicked loose by a climber above, it could mean death for a climber below. In fact, as the fifth climber from the top, I was fearful.

And just then. Just as I was thinking about the danger of rock fall, I heard someone scream, "ROCK!" Followed by a BANG, BANG, BANG! To reduce my exposure to the falling rock, I tucked up against the chute's right wall. BANG, BANG! There was the rock, whizzing by me. Oh man, that rock was the size of my head!

I was about to shout up to ask if everyone were OK, when again I heard, BANG, BANG, BANG! And again a scream, "ROCK!" BANG, BANG, BANG! This time, more than one rock came down. Three or four I think.

Then quiet.

I called up, "Is everyone OK? Everyone, from the bottom up, call down to me. Are each of you OK?"

One by one, each responded. One said he was so frightened he couldn't move. I told him to stay where he was. And I asked everyone to be quiet, because I wanted to speak with Eddie. Eddie answered. He said something about the route may be going to the top though it seemed difficult. I told him I didn't care about difficulty, instead I was thinking about safety. And that our attempt to climb Mount Sill had come to an end. All that mattered was getting the group back down out of the chute safely.

I guess I just kind of took charge. I called up to the climbers in the chute. From their response, I learned that the fellow who was too frightened to move was second in line, with only Eddie up above him. And that he was in a relatively safe position. He was tucked under a ledge, so that if a rock were to fall from above, he'd likely be OK.

I called to the two climbers below him and told them to climb down slowly, one at a time, beginning with the person at the bottom. Yes, it was a slow way to get the group out of the chute, but it was the safest way. With only Eddie and the frightened fellow remaining in the chute, Eddie could climb down to help him. And that's what he did. As each of the climbers came out from the bottom of the chute, their facial expressions clearly conveyed fear. One of the climbers exclaimed, "Man, we were seriously off route. That stupid chute isn't a route to anything except trouble. We're lucky to step away from that chute alive."

It was turning cooler as we walked back down the glacier. We hiked to the saddle and, from there, to the top of the rock wall. The climb down the route we had previously come up appeared very difficult. So we looked for an alternate route.

As we had little daylight remaining, we broke into parties of three or four climbers, each party finding its own route to descend the wall. By doing so, each three-party team could descend more quickly than were our full party of fifteen to use the same route.

Two other climbers and I stayed close to our up-route. But there, the down climb looked difficult, so we decided to rappel (to slowly slide down the rope). We set up an anchor and threw the rappel rope over the top of the wall. But the height of the wall exceeded the length of the rope, so we'd have to take it in two rappels. Or descend elsewhere. OK, I'd pull the rope back up. But the rope snagged in a crack, and try as I did, I couldn't get it free. It was getting dark. We had to get going. I had no choice but to abandon the rope.

But having left the rope, we'd lost our ability to rappel, or to belay (to protect a climber by tying into the rope). It was quickly growing darker; we'd have to commit to one route or another pretty soon. We found a route with which we felt somewhat more comfortable. Not that we were comfortable, we were just less uncomfortable. More than a bit nervous, we did manage to climb down.

It was dark when we arrived in camp. Though tired, we were all safe and sound. Not an injury in the entire party. We were lucky. Back up there in the chute, a handful of us were certainly in a position where we could easily have been killed.

We ate a quick dinner and crawled into our sleeping bags. About sunrise the next morning, we ate breakfast, broke camp, and hiked down the long granite slab to Third Lake. And out to our cars.

The next summer, Jack Cole and Dave Franzen returned to climb Mount Sill. They again camped below the rock wall, climbed up the wall to the saddle, and skirted the bottom edge of the glacier to the first chute—the one I argued for a year earlier. They reported that the climb up to the summit was pretty straightforward. A bit spooky in just one place near the top, but a really fun climb.

As for me, no, I've never been on the summit of Mount Sill. ➤

Chapter 11

Have You Seen My Partner?

I N THE SUMMER OF 1972, I sold my old Chevy sedan. The buyer lived in Oceanside, some eighty miles south of my home in Fullerton, about half way to the Mexican border. He asked me to deliver the car and I told him I would. I figured that hitchhiking home might offer an interesting adventure. Indeed it did.

I drove to Oceanside, delivered the car, signed over the registration form, and put $650 cash into the left front pocket of my jeans. Then I walked over to Highway 76 and stuck out my thumb. Before long, a station wagon stopped to pick me up. It was a Mexican-American family—Mom, Dad and three small kids. Nice folks. Good thing I could speak Spanish, because these folks spoke not a word of English. They told me they were sorry they couldn't take me farther, but they weren't going north as I was. They dropped me at the on-ramp to the 5 Freeway. I stepped out of the car and, once again, stuck out my thumb.

Traffic was light. I stood there for well over an hour. And those drivers that did whiz by, barely looked my way. The sun was setting. I glanced at my watch—8:15. I thought, *It's even less likely that someone will stop for me in the dark.*

Just then, a small white car rolled to a stop. As the driver was alone in the car, I opened the front passenger door and sat down next to him.

Have you ever looked at someone and just known, intuitively, that they were up to no good? Well that was the feeling I had about the driver. He had a stocky build and wore a black leather jacket. And a black leather cap with a small brim pulled down low over his eyes. He made a sort of a "click" sound out of the right side of his mouth at the end of each sentence. Happy as I was to be headed toward home, I felt a bit uneasy.

He seemed friendly enough. In fact, he was quite talkative. He asked my name and where I was from, and what I did for a living. I answered his questions. Then he asked, "What were you doing down in Oceanside?"

I told him, "I sold my car to a fellow in Oceanside. Now I'm on the way home."

As I said that, I realized I'd made a mistake. For knowing I'd just sold my car, he'd assume that I would be carrying cash. So I hastened to add, "The car was an old jalopy. It hardly ran at all."

Purposely changing the subject, I asked, "What's your name?"

He said, "You can call me Mitch."

"What do you do for a living, Mitch?"

He told me, "I smuggle illegal aliens into the country. We have three in the trunk of this car right now."

I thought, *Hell, I'm not about to believe that story. Certainly if it were true, he wouldn't tell me about it. And besides this stupid little car wouldn't even fit three people in the trunk.*

Then he said, "I picked you up because the Border Patrol wouldn't expect a smuggler to have a passenger inside the car. Actually, you're my decoy."

Yeah, sure, I figured. By then, I was really worried. While I certainly didn't believe his ridiculous story about three guys in the trunk, I didn't trust this fellow. I began to wonder if I might be in danger.

Before too long, we came to the Border Patrol inspection station. The officer waved us right through. Then Mitch asked me, "Have you seen my partner?"

"Have I seen your partner? No, I don't know who your partner is." I replied. Actually, I thought his question was preposterous. How in the world was I supposed to know anything about his partner?

"Well," he said, "we'd better stop to find my partner."

Oh-oh, I thought. *Now I'm really worried.* I wasn't especially interested in his partner. Not half so much as I was interested in arriving home safely.

We approached the exit at San Juan Capistrano. "We'll get off here and look for my partner," Mitch said.

I figured, *Oh-oh, this can't be good.*

Near the freeway exit was a Colony Kitchen, a combination restaurant-motel. The restaurant, in the front of the building, was well-lit. I assumed that Mitch would drive up to the restaurant and park the car. Then I'd simply walk into the well-lit, hopefully well-populated restaurant, and not return to his car.

But Mitch drove up, not to the well-lit front of the building, but to the very dark rear of the building. My heart pounded and my mind raced with a terrible thought: *If I'm going to find trouble this evening, it will be right here in back of this building.*

As the car rolled to a stop, I reached for the doorknob with my right hand. I planned to spring out of the car and make a run for it. But before I could open the door, Mitch grabbed my left wrist firmly. "Just a minute. Let me tell the boys in the trunk that we're stopping here."

Surprised by what he was telling me, I turned to look at him.

In Spanish, Mitch said in a loud voice, "We're stopping here for just a little while. Then we'll proceed directly to Los Angeles. Don't move and don't say anything."

As soon as he finished offering that instruction, a voice from the trunk of the car replied, "Muy bien."

Oh my gosh. I thought. *There really are some guys in the trunk! Mitch really is a smuggler. He's not a mugger. Well then, I'm in no danger at all.*

I relaxed completely. I felt elated. Ready for a celebration. Speaking of celebration, it turned out that in the rear of that building was a bar. Apparently, that was where Mitch would look for his partner. He asked me, "Are you ready for a beer?"

"Man, am I!"

Firmly planted on a bar stool, I reached into my pocket—not the left pocket with 650 dollars in it—but instead the right pocket containing 9 dollars. I slapped the nine bucks down on the bar. But Mitch waved his hand in front of me ordering, "Put your money away. This is a business expense. I'm buying the beer."

Man, that first sip tasted great!

About the time I took my second sip, a tall, thin fellow walked into the bar carrying a large suitcase. Funny thing about that suitcase, in spite of its size, it was, apparently, very light. Because holding it in one hand, the tall fellow stood up absolutely straight without straining in the least.

Spotting him, Mitch called out, "Hey, Tony. Psst. Tony. Over here."

Glancing my way, Mitch said, "That's my partner."

"Yeah, I figured."

Tony walked up to join us at the bar. Waving toward me, he asked, "Hey, who's he?"

"It's OK, he's a friend."

Yeah, I thought, *I'm a friend.*

Mitch suggested, "Let's go sit in that back corner booth."

We walked to the back corner of the bar far away from everyone else.

Near that booth, up against the wall, there was plenty of room for Tony to place his suitcase. But he didn't place it there. Instead, he lifted it over the table and set it on the bench. Then he slid across the bench and kind of snuggled up against his suitcase. I thought, *Whatever is in that suitcase, Tony cares about it a whole lot.*

So we sat drinking beer, this smuggler of illegal aliens, his suitcase toting partner and I. For ten minutes, maybe fifteen, the two of them chatted about things of no consequence whatsoever. I sat quietly, sipping my beer, and thinking, *Nobody is going to believe this story.*

When we finished our beer, we walked out to the car and hopped in, Tony up front with Mitch, and I in the back seat wedged between Tony's suitcase and the right rear window. *That's strange,* I thought. *Tony is coming along with us. But I assumed he'd have his own car. If not, then how in the world did he and his suitcase arrive at the bar?*

Before starting the engine, Mitch announced, in Spanish, "We're back now and we'll proceed directly to Los Angeles."

This time, I wasn't at all surprised when a voice from behind me replied, "Muy bien."

Traveling north on the 5 Freeway, Mitch and Tony spoke of cars having large engines, those cars able to outrun other cars when necessary. Having little to add to their conversation, I sat quietly. I remember looking at Tony's suitcase and thinking, *I'd sure like to take a little peak inside.* But I dared not. And besides, it was probably locked.

They dropped me off at Harbor Boulevard, near Disneyland. I stepped out of the car and thanked Mitch for the ride and for the beer. I watched the little white car re-enter the freeway and disappear into a long ribbon of red lights.

I was then just four miles from home. Again, I stuck out my thumb. Within just a few minutes, a small dark-colored car stopped to pick me up.

The driver, a youngish fellow, about my age, was alone in the car. So I sat down in the front passenger seat.

He was actually quite talkative. In fact, he was extremely friendly. He asked me lots of questions. But it was his last question which took me by surprise. He asked, "What kind of underwear do you wear, trunks or briefs?"

Ever so slowly, I turned to look at him. I remember thinking, *nobody is going to believe this story*. But of course, I didn't tell him that. I simply said, "Look I'm really tired. How about we just travel along silently and you drop me off at Orangethorpe Avenue. OK?"

He didn't reply. In fact, neither of us said another word for the remainder of the trip. Arriving at Orangethorpe Avenue, I stepped out of the car and said, "Thank you."

He said, "You're welcome."

Then, just a few blocks from home, I traveled the rest of the way on foot. I remember walking along slowly, shaking my head from side to side, and repeating over and over, "Nobody is going to believe this story." ➤

Part Three

Two Special Places

WHILE A YOUNG MAN living in California, I became enamored with adventuring in two special places. So I returned to both of them again and again. The first of those special places was Baja California, Mexico—the thousand-mile-long peninsula stretching south from the U.S. State of California. With a backbone of high mountains, Baja California is bordered on the west by the Pacific Ocean and on the east by the Sea of Cortez. Geographically separated from mainland Mexico, it has traditionally been isolated from the political and social problems of the rest of the nation. Deserts, mountains, unpaved roads, and friendly people—what more could an adventurer ask for?

My second special place was Toroweap Point, an especially remote and spectacularly beautiful spot on the Grand Canyon's north rim. Red cliffs dotted with green vegetation, a lava spill offering a steep descent to the Colorado River, and all of it untouched by time. Plus the friendship of the ranger who lived there alone. No wonder I returned there again and again.

Chapter 12

Dirty Dan

I N THE FALL OF 1969, we flew down to Mexico's Baja California peninsula in a twin engine, private plane. The occasion was the Baja 1,000
race. A hundred or so four-wheel drive cars, dune buggies, and motorcycles would bounce along the one-thousand-mile, torturous, dusty trail
between Ensenada and La Paz.

I was accompanied by three others. There was my roommate, Gary,
who was always ready for an adventure. And Ernie, a freelance photographer on assignment to shoot pictures of the race for *Road and Track*
magazine. And there was our pilot, Dirty Dan, who Gary introduced me
to that very morning. Dan got the "Dirty" part of his name because he
owned a topless bar in Los Angeles.

It was warm that afternoon when we boarded the twin engine, six seat
airplane at Fullerton Airport. We had a smooth flight down to the agricultural border town of Mexicali where we had dinner and spent the night in
a small, non-memorable motel. The next morning, we got an early start
flying across the mountains to Ensenada where the race would begin.

While flying over the mountains, Dan provided us with an early morning surprise. I'm sure he considered it a funny little joke, but to Gary, Ernie,
and me, it was terrifying. He shut off the fuel flow to one of the engines,

so while a thousand feet above the mountains, the engine stopped. While pulling this stunt, he acted alarmed, as if to frighten us. Then once assured that he had successfully scared the hell out of us, he chuckled and calmly restarted the engine. We didn't know it at the time, but this early morning dose of terror was actually a clue to what we would experience later that same day.

We landed at Ensenada Airport and bummed a ride in a vegetable truck up to the start of the race. There we watched as, one by one, the four-wheelers, dune buggies, and motorcycles leapt off the starting line. After we had watched thirty or so vehicles roar away, each additional vehicle's start seemed pretty repetitive. Even Ernie began to wonder just how many starting line shots he might sell to *Road and Track* magazine. So we decided to return to the airplane and fly about halfway down the peninsula where we would land at a little village called El Arco to watch the racers roar by in the dust.

But just before we left the starting line, a scantily dressed, curvaceous, blond-haired gal showed up and greeted Dan with a friendly hug. Dan introduced her as a gal who worked in his topless bar.

"Hi boys," she said, "I'm Cupcakes."

"Hi, Cupcakes."

Gary looked at me as if to ask, "Is this gal for real?"

I hadn't the slightest idea how Cupcakes got down to Ensenada, but Dan said she'd be coming along with us. So we'd now be five in the airplane.

The plane had three rows of seats, each two across. Dan, as our pilot, sat front left. Gary sat front right next to Dan. I sat mid-left behind Dan, and Cupcakes sat to my right. Ernie sat rear-left behind me, and he used the rear-right seat for his photo equipment.

We took off and Dan pointed us south, down the peninsula. Ernie, sitting behind me, tapped me on the shoulder and shouted, "Ask Dan if we could fly north a bit. I want to get some aerial shots of the starting line."

It was difficult to communicate above the noise of the engines, so I leaned forward, tapped Dan on the shoulder, and shouted, "Ernie would like to fly back up north to get some pictures of the starting line."

"Sure thing," said Dan. With that, he turned the plane around in a way that, to say the least, commanded our attention. He rolled the plane over on its side so that the left wing tip pointed straight down toward the ground. Then he kind of spun the plane around so I could look straight out of my window, past the left wing tip, and watch the ground rotating clockwise.

As I don't do too terribly well with motion, this little antic made my stomach feel pretty uneasy. Seated behind Dan, I couldn't tell if he were smiling, but I sure suspected so. Again he was having his little joke on us. I glanced around to see both Gary and Cupcakes holding on tight. Then I turned back to check on Ernie. He was staring ahead blankly and looking especially pale.

Dan leveled out the plane and headed north back toward the starting line. About half a minute later, Ernie tapped me on the shoulder and shouted in my ear, "Dan isn't going to do that again, is he?"

My stomach still feeling uneasy, I answered, "I hope not."

Within a few minutes we were back at the starting line. And again Dan rolled the plane. I looked over the left wing tip straight down at the ground. Yep, there was the starting line rotating clockwise. Trying not to think about our spinning around as we were, I turned back to look at Ernie. I wondered if he were getting some good aerial shots of the starting line. No, he wasn't. Again staring blankly, he hadn't even raised his camera. Instead it remained firmly planted in his lap.

Dan leveled the plane and headed south.

For the next two hours or so, we flew by the racers as they bounced along the ground in a cloud of dust. Dan periodically swooped down for a closer look. I'm sure this swooping wasn't particularly safe, but it was exciting and we enjoyed it. At times we got so close that the racers would look up at us in amazement.

But all of this swooping was taking its toll on Ernie. He hadn't yet recovered from Dan's earlier aerobatic entertainment. It seemed to me a very real possibility that Ernie might soon become ill. I told this to the others and we all agreed that landing the plane pretty soon would be a good idea.

Fortunately, we were close to El Arco, our mid-peninsula destination. Within another ten minutes or so, we spotted the airfield. Typical of most runways in Baja California, this one was unpaved. Worse than that, it was on a hill, so it was higher in the middle and lower at both ends. That would make for a pretty tough landing, especially for our larger twin engine plane. And with the front half of the runway going uphill, it would be tough to touch down near the start of the runway. To make matters even worse, we had a pretty stiff crosswind gusting from the left.

With my pilot friend, Jim Hammond, I had done some traveling by small plane in Baja California. So I knew that, when landing on a dirt runway, it was a good idea—in fact, a *very* good idea—to do a "fly by." That means, before landing, to first fly low over the runway looking for potholes. Well guess what? Dan didn't do a fly by. Instead, he immediately put us on approach to land. I leaned forward and shouted, "Hey Dan, aren't you going to fly by once and look for potholes?"

"No," was his quick reply.

As we approached the runway, we could feel a stiff gust pushing the plane to the right. Dan struggled to keep the plane level and pointed straight ahead. Then I noticed yet another problem. We were coming in "late." That is, we were flying by the front half of the runway and would touch down near the top of the hill. That would leave us just the second half of the runway on which to land a large, twin engine plane. And that second half of the runway was downhill!

I leaned forward and shouted, "Hey Dan, aren't we coming in late? Shouldn't we go back around and make another approach?"

Dan waved his hand back toward my face and yelled, "Leave me alone, I'm flying this plane."

Well, that was it. I tried. There was nothing more I could do but hope for the best. As we came closer to the ground, I watched more and more of the runway disappearing behind us. We touched down mid-runway, just about at the top of the hill. The dirt landing strip was fairly smooth, so potholes weren't the problem. The problem was stopping a large, twin engine plane on the downhill half of the runway.

Once on the ground, the big plane rolled and rolled and rolled and kept on rolling. As we neared the end of the runway with just fifty feet to go, we were still rolling about forty miles an hour. I was sure that we'd run off the end of the runway and bust up the plane amongst cactus and rocks. So I grabbed Cupcakes around the shoulders, threw her head into my lap, and rolled my upper body over her head and shoulders.

About then, Dan figured out we were in trouble, so he did what I suppose was an emergency maneuver. He turned the plane hard to the left putting us into a sideways skid. Instead of running nose first across a hundred feet of desert, we skidded to an abrupt stop about twenty feet beyond the end of the runway. We kicked up so much dust that we couldn't see a thing outside of the plane.

As we screeched to a stop, our one door, on the right side of the plane, flew open. Realizing that leaking fuel and a resultant fire were real possibilities, we quickly scurried down from the plane and backed off some thirty feet or so. It took a few minutes for the dust to settle; when it finally did, we were able to access the damage. Fortunately, nothing major. The door had flown open because our skid had twisted the fuselage. So we would continue our trip with the door wired in an "almost closed" position. Our skid had also stressed our right tire so it had developed a rather large bubble. Thus a potential blowout on our next landing. And our right propeller had struck the ground, so its blade tips were well dented.

All in all, we were lucky. Five well-shaken passengers, but no injuries. And the plane still sort of flyable. With the help of two local quasi-mechanics, we hammered the propeller tips back into a reasonable condition.

About two hours later, we took off and headed south toward La Paz. There we could get the plane repaired. For sure a new tire. Maybe even a new propeller.

Flying in the same plane had become far less comfortable. The door wired in an "almost closed" position produced a loud whistling sound. So we could no longer communicate by shouting. Instead we resorted to hand signals and gestures. And our dented up, hammered-nearly-into-shape propeller was considerably out of balance. This offered a significant vibration.

As irritating as the whistle and the vibration were, we worried most about the threat laying silent and motionless beneath us. Would our damaged tire survive one more landing? Or would it blow out as we touched down in La Paz?

We got lucky. No blowout upon landing. We taxied over to the airport's service center where we delivered the plane for repairs. Then we hopped in a taxi and headed to town.

Staring out the window of the taxi, I thought of something that my very cautious pilot friend, Jim Hammond, once told me, "There are old pilots and there are bold pilots. But there are no old, bold pilots." Dirty Dan was still a young pilot. I was happy to be on the ground. ➤

Chapter 13

Baja by 4-Wheel Drive

I N THE FALL OF 1970, Jim Peterson and I spent three glorious weeks touring the Baja California peninsula. At the time, the Mexican government was just beginning to pave Baja's main road. And since even the peninsula's main road was more accurately described as a rough trail, we expected the trip to be very much an "expedition." We'd travel in "The Tank," my 1968 four-wheel-drive Toyota Landcruiser.

Jim didn't concern himself too much about planning for the trip. Oh sure, he helped me install the extra gas tank in the Landcruiser. And he helped box and load the motor oil and spare parts. But he didn't concern himself too much with learning about the people, the economy, the landscape, the vegetation, and the language of the peninsula. In a way, I admired his relaxed attitude. And his ability to kind of take life as it came.

I, on the other hand, prepared fully for our expedition. I had been studying the language for a number of years. And I had read about the economy, topography, culture, vegetation, and the people. I even attended a UCLA extension course, "The Flora and Fauna of Baja California."

Wanting to fully experience our adventure, we removed the top and the doors from the Landcruiser. Thus we'd be totally exposed to the weather. We also removed the rear seats. Doing so offered more space for our four duffle bags, two sleeping bags, two boxes of auto and food supplies, and cooking gear.

The extra gas tank we installed offered a driving range of about four hundred miles. Somewhat less, of course, on the rough, dirt roads. Spare headlamps, motor oil, clothing, and snorkel diving equipment all packed aboard. And, oh yes, water bottles. A five-gallon steel can attached to either side of our topless truck.

I got my hair cut short and planted a straw cowboy hat on my head. And a smile on my face. I had been looking forward to this trip for a very long time.

Our first adventure was our visit to El Mármol. El Mármol, "marble" in English, is the name of a mine. It isn't really marble they mine at El Mármol, but rather a type of onyx that resembles marble. I had read that there was a house built entirely of onyx up at the mine. This sounded pretty interesting so we decided to drive up to take a look.

A terribly rocky road led up to El Mármol. Actually, it was hardly a road, but more like a trail just wide enough for a truck. As I recall, we traveled for a couple of hours and gained perhaps a thousand feet in elevation.

Arriving on top of a broad hill, we saw a large clearing to our left. It looked like a landing strip. And there was a wind sock. I asked, "Hey Jim, why in the world would anyone build an airstrip way up here?"

Jim guessed, "Maybe to deliver food and supplies to the miners."

"But that doesn't make sense," I responded. "The trucks that carry onyx down the hill could carry food and supplies back up the hill."

"Then why the airstrip?" we wondered.

A bit further along the road, we arrived in a broad valley. There to our right, we saw two small storage sheds. And about a hundred yards away was the onyx house. But before we could even say, "there it is," the door to the onyx house flew open. Out came two men running toward our truck. They were carrying rifles.

I stopped the truck, turned off the ignition, and stepped out on the driver side. Jim stepped out on the passenger side. The two men, now standing in front of our truck, were pointing their rifles toward us. I guess they figured we couldn't speak Spanish, because they didn't say anything. Speaking first, I said, "Buenas tardes" (Good afternoon). They seemed relieved to learn we could communicate. But they kept their rifles pointed toward us.

They asked, in Spanish of course, "What do you have in the back of your truck?"

I told them, "We have food, clothing, camping supplies, and snorkel diving equipment."

One of them said, "We'll take a look."

All four of us walked around to the rear of the truck. Jim removed the canvas tarp that covered our gear. We had been using the tarp in a hopeless attempt to keep our gear dust-free. We quickly learned, however, that on this trip keeping anything dust-free was impossible.

One of the men slapped the sides of a couple of our duffle bags. Each slap seemed to satisfy him until he got to one particular duffle bag. I think he hit something solid. He asked, "What is in this bag?"

I replied, "It's our snorkel diving equipment. Would you like me to open the bag for you?"

He said, "No."

The other man with a rifle pointed toward us asked, "Do you have any guns?"

"No," I answered.

Then, that same man asked us, "Would you like a cup of coffee?"

I smiled and answered, "Yes."

The two fellows pointed their rifles down toward the ground—which pleased both Jim and me—and walked toward the onyx house. We followed along.

Yes, it really was a house made entirely of onyx. It looked pretty much like marble except for the greenish color. And most of the rock was rough. Like it had been chipped out of much larger pieces. It seemed to me that a person could get cut just leaning against the wall.

Inside the house were four steel-framed beds. Each was covered by a not-very-clean, beat-up mattress. A single small table completed the furniture collection. The table was covered with sacks of rice, beans and coffee, and some canned vegetables. Slabs of meat hung from the ceiling.

The four of us sat down on two of the bunks facing toward each other. We each held a cup of coffee in our lap. It was then I remembered that I don't drink coffee. I drank it that day.

We visited for about a half hour. From our hosts we learned the purpose of the airstrip. Seems that a number of American hunters had been coming down to the mountains of Baja California to hunt the bighorn sheep, an animal the Mexican Government had designated protected. And El Mármol was right in the middle of the bighorn sheep's range. So the government had stationed soldiers at El Mármol and built the airstrip to fly in soldiers and supplies. Two soldiers at a time would live in the onyx house for a few days; then two more would fly in to relieve them.

No, I didn't ask what they would have done with us if we'd had rifles. I didn't even want to think about it. Besides, why ruin such a nice visit?

Maybe, in my whole life, I've had a dozen cups of coffee. That cup of coffee in El Mármol's onyx house was, by far, the most memorable.

A Beer Beside the Stream

About three days after leaving El Mármol we arrived in the village of San Ignacio. It's probably much changed today, but back then the town was a pretty, peaceful community of small farm plots and goat ranches. A stream ran through the town and along the stream was a fair-sized grove of date palm trees. We found San Ignacio to be a pleasant oasis in the middle of the hot, dry desert.

Entering town from the north, we noticed a cluster of straw huts to our right. We didn't know it at the time, but we would sleep in one of those huts for the next three nights.

We passed a few small houses on the left. Children and dogs playing in a dry, dusty backyard. Flowerpots made from old tires. I remember thinking that in poor communities such as this, nothing goes to waste.

We drove over a small bridge crossing the stream. Then through a date palm grove. We were surprised at how much cooler it was under the date palm trees. The beauty of traveling with the top off the Landcruiser was that we were right out there in the weather. Able to enjoy, or suffer from, our immediate surroundings.

Another half mile perhaps and we arrived in the middle of the village. A quiet little plaza. A food store and a small snack shop. And a general store that served as both hardware store and gas station. We filled up with gasoline, which we pumped out of a barrel and through a cloth filter. Both Jim and I were surprised at the amount of rust that had accumulated in the cloth filter.

I asked the fellow in the general store if there were a hotel in San Ignacio. He directed me to the cluster of straw huts at the north end of town—those which we had driven by about an hour earlier. He said that the Nuñez family would charge fifty cents American per night for use of a hut. Plus another fifty cents for a shower. And, if we chose to, we could also eat our meals with the family in their home. As this description sounded interesting, we drove north, headed for the Nuñez home and cluster of straw huts.

We came to the small bridge that crossed the stream by the date palm grove. There along the stream and adjacent the grove, we saw a small shack with a sign which read, "Cantina." We both smiled thinking about the opportunity to drink a beer. A medium-sized man in a light blue shirt was moving some boxes out behind the shack.

We pulled off the road, stopped the engine, and walked up to the shack. The man seemed apprehensive, probably concerned that we'd have trouble communicating with him. So I said, "Buenas tardes". He offered a broad smile and repeated, "Buenas tardes."

I asked, "Is the beer cold?"

He said, "Yes." But somehow his answer seemed unconvincing.

Jim reminded me, "When you're really thirsty, don't get too hung up about the temperature of the beer. Rather, take pleasure in the fact that it's wet."

I figured this was one such occasion.

We asked for two beers, then walked a few paces down to the stream, sat on the ground, and began drinking them. The man got a beer for himself, came over to the stream, and sat down beside us. He asked us a bunch of questions. Like, "Where are you going?" "What route have you driven?" And "How come you're going all the way down the peninsula?"

We answered each of his questions.

Before we had a chance to ask him much about San Ignacio, a taxicab arrived. The driver, a very large man, stepped out from the cab, helped himself to a beer, and joined us by the stream.

During our visit by the stream, these two locals found out quite a bit about us. And from these two locals, we learned quite a bit about San Ignacio. For one, the town had grown quite a bit during the 1960s. So its only electric generator was no longer large enough to provide power to the entire populace. Each day, the power distribution would switch from one half of town to the other. Then back again on the next day.

We also found out that there was a second taxi in town, piloted by a woman driver. Except she was in jail. Seems that, a few days earlier, she got drunk and drove her taxi off the bridge and into the stream. So the police put her in jail to teach her a lesson.

I really don't recall how long we spent visiting by the stream that afternoon. And I don't remember how much not very cold beer we drank. All I can tell you is that it was one of the most peaceful afternoons I've ever spent—ever. Just sitting there visiting, and laying back on the grass under the trees. Not concerned about accomplishing anything. Or getting anywhere. Just being.

After traveling in rural Mexico for a few days, the world slows way down. And any haste or stress the traveler might have brought along with him simply evaporates. That's what happened for Jim and me, that afternoon in San Ignacio.

Two Old Guys on Motorcycles

About the middle of the next morning, two dust-covered motorcycles sporting Arizona license plates roared into town. Both motorcycles carried riders who looked quite a bit older than my vision of dirt bikers.

In a small Mexican village, you get to know all the travelers after a day or two. So we figured that we'd soon learn about these two dust-covered, older fellows. Sure enough, that same evening, we ate dinner, in the Nuñez home, with the newly arrived Gringos. Following dinner, I spoke privately with the younger of the two. Turns out he was fifty-six years old. He told me that he was taking the trip mainly to look after his older companion who was seventy-three years old.

Later, I chatted privately with the older man. He had wonderful stories to tell about his motorcycle trips to remote places during the prior four decades. Good long rides, mainly on dirt roads and trails. Some by himself, some with traveling companions. He wore a broad smile and his eyes sparkled as he told stories of his adventures in both North and South

America. Then, after about fifteen minutes of joyful storytelling, he turned sad. "But I think this will be my last motorcycle trip," he said.

His remark, along with the look of sadness on his face, made me feel sorry for him. Not knowing exactly what to say, I broke the uncomfortable silence with the awkward comment, "Well, I guess we all have to quit sometime."

"Oh no," he quickly replied, "I'm not quitting because of me. It's my wife. The poor dear worries so." ➢

Chapter 14

Towing a Twin Engine Plane

JIM AND I HAD BEEN EXPECTING our friends Bob and Carl, from Colorado Springs, to arrive in San Ignacio during the next day or two. They were coming down to preview the road on which they'd race in the Baja 1,000 just one week later. Having arrived during the night while Jim and I were asleep, they recognized my Landcruiser and bedded down in the straw hut next to ours.

Since they arrived quite late, both Bob and Carl were still asleep at nine the next morning. Having just finished breakfast in the Nuñez family's home, Jim and I returned to our hut to rearrange some gear. It was then that we heard an airplane flying low over the village. Jim said, "That plane sounds low enough to be landing."

We hurried out from the hut just in time to glimpse a twin engine plane flying low over the treetops. I said, "Looks like he's headed toward the dry lake, Laguna San Ignacio."

Jim said, "He'd better not land on the dry lake. That lake has just a few inches of dry soil on top with wet soil beneath. If he tries to land on it, he'll sink the plane in up to its axels."

Awakened by the sound of the plane, Bob and Carl were then emerging from their hut. "Was that Dirty Dan?" Bob asked.

"We're not sure," I replied, "Let's go take a look."

Jim and I got into the Landcruiser and drove out toward Laguna San Ignacio. Bob and Carl followed in their truck. Fortunately, there was a not-terribly-bumpy dirt road along the edge of the dry lake. I drove while Jim looked out onto the dry lake for a glimpse of the twin engine plane. After about ten minutes, Jim spotted the plane. "There it is, off in the distance," he said pointing.

As we approached the plane, we could see that it had sunk into the wet sandy soil up to its axels—just as Jim had predicted. "Hey, look," shouted Jim, "The door is opening."

We then saw the plane's door open downward exposing the ladder that was built into the inside of the door. We rolled to a stop on the road, some fifty yards from the plane. I turned off the engine.

Jim said, "Look, there's Dan."

I looked up to see Dirty Dan coming out from the plane and onto the ladder. He stepped down the ladder and onto the surface of the dry lake. "Look Jim," I said, "Good thing the dry surface is able to support his weight."

As Bob's truck rolled to a stop behind ours, he exclaimed, "Look, there's a girl coming down the ladder. Must be one of the gals from Dan's bar."

We watched as, to our surprise, not one, not two, but five scantily clad girls, one by one, stepped down the ladder and onto the surface of the dry lake. "Now isn't that a sight? Jim said. "Who else but Dirty Dan would bring a handful of gals from his topless bar onto a dry lake in the middle of the Baja California peninsula? And he's even got 'em dressed like hookers. And to top it all off, he goes and sinks his twin engine plane up to its axels in the lake."

I agreed, "Yeah, an odd site. But now that he's sunk up to his axels, I suppose we'll have to help him get out."

With that, Bob, Carl, Jim, and I left the two vehicles on the road and walked out onto the lake and toward Dan's plane. "Good morning, Dan," said Carl.

"Good morning, guys.

Two or three of the gals said "Hello." Two or three of them giggled. And a couple of them discovered that the surface of the dry lake wouldn't support high-heeled shoes. Removing their shoes, they giggled about the odd feeling of cold sand on the bottom of their feet.

Jim was right; this really was quite a sight. I asked, "Hey Dan, how come you landed here on the lake?"

He replied, "Well, Carl had told me that you guys would be meeting in San Ignacio, so I thought I'd drop in and join the party. And with no airport close by, this lake seemed a likely place to land. I wanted to ask you when you'll be arriving in La Paz. I thought that perhaps we could meet there. You know, dinner or drinks or something."

Bob looked down at the plane's wheels sunk in the wet sand and asked, "Say Dan, do you think you could rev up your engines to free the plane's wheels?"

"Oh yeah, I'm sure I can do that with no problem."

I turned to Jim and said quietly, "I'm not so sure he'll be able to."

Jim whispered, "Neither am I."

So we all visited for a while and talked about maybe meeting up in La Paz. Dinner or drinks, as Dan suggested. Then Dan climbed back up the ladder and into the plane. The girls followed, waving and giggling.

Carl said, "Good luck getting out of the wet sand."

Bob, Carl, Jim, and I walked back to the road as Dan started up the plane's twin engines. Then he gunned the throttle and the plane made a heck of a roar. The props whirled and a whole lot of dry surface sand flew into the air behind the plane.

But the plane didn't move at all. The wheels were buried too far into the wet sand beneath the surface of the lake. Clearly Dan was wrong; revving up the engines wouldn't pull the plane from the dry lake. He was seriously stuck.

Bob then suggested, "Hey, Bill, how about you try towing the plane? If you put the Landcruiser in four-wheel drive and in your lowest gear, I'll bet you could pull the plane from the dry lake. Of course Dan would rev up his engines at the same time."

"Sure worth a try," I replied. Then, turning to Dan, I added, "Say Dan, when the plane starts moving, make sure you don't run over me in the Landcruiser."

"Wouldn't think of it," replied Dan.

But he had this funny looking grin on his face, which I interpreted as his thinking that running over me with a twin engine airplane might actually be fun. So I made sure to select the longer of the two towropes from Bob's truck.

I put the Landcruiser into four-wheel drive and drove out onto the dry lake. Fortunately, the dry surface of the lake held up under the vehicle's weight. *Good*, I thought. *I certainly don't need to get the Landcruiser stuck too.*

We tied one end of the rope to the Landcruiser's frame and the other to the plane's landing gear. Dan revved up his engines, the props spun, and the plane made a heck of a roar. Then, in my very lowest gear, I applied the gas and began to move forward just a bit. But not very far. Just far enough to stretch the rope.

And then, I felt the Landcruiser sinking. I quickly lifted my foot from the accelerator and shifted into neutral. I stepped out from the Landcruiser to see just how far I'd buried the tires in the sand. Fortunately, I had sunk the tires into the sand just four or five inches. Not very bad. Once untying the tow rope I'd be able to drive out.

OK, so that idea didn't work. I bent down to untie the rope from the Landcruiser's frame when Bob said, "Hey Bill, I've got another idea."

"What is it?" I asked.

Pointing up the hill beyond the road, Bob suggested, "Do you see all that driftwood up on the hill? How about we use driftwood to build two tracks for the Landcruiser's wheels? That should keep it from breaking through the dry surface of the lake. And we could cut the metal bed liner out of my pickup truck to build skids for the wheels of the plane. Using those skids, we should be able to raise the wheels of the plane up onto the dry surface of the lake."

Then Jim asked, "But what about when the plane's wheels reach the end of the skids. Won't the wheels, once again, sink through the surface of the lake?"

Bob, who apparently had been thinking about this plan for a while, quickly answered, "We'll prepare two sets of skids for the plane's wheels. While the wheels are traveling on one set of skids, we'll place a second set of skids out in front. Then when the wheels are traveling on the second set of skids, we'll move the first set from behind the wheels to the front. We'll need four people for this task."

Bob went on to explain, "Same thing with the Landcruiser. As Bill drives along on the driftwood tracks, a team of four can move driftwood from behind the Landcruiser to the front."

This sounded like a pretty good plan. And besides, we had no other ideas. So we quickly got about setting up this scheme that Bob suggested. Jim and I drove the Landcruiser up the hill and filled it with a bunch of driftwood. Then we drove back down to the lake and solicited the help of the girls to create two driftwood tracks out in front of the Landcruiser. My team included Jim plus three girls who giggled while working enthusiastically. Clearly, they were enjoying a wonderful adventure.

Bob and Carl dug into their toolbox and found a pair of metal-cutting shears. They used the shears to create four skids from the steel bed liner of their truck.

Then, all of us working together, dug out a bunch of sand from in front of the plane's wheels. We tucked the steel skids up against the front of the wheels.

Skids in place, driftwood tracks in place, rope tied from Landcruiser to airplane, we were ready. Again, I started up the Landcruiser and put it in my very lowest gear. Again, Dan revved up the airplane's engines kicking up a bunch of sand. Jim and three of the girls stood ready to move driftwood from the rear to the front of the Landcruiser. Carl, Bob, and two of the girls stood ready to move one set of skids from the back to the front of the plane's wheels.

Rrrr ... grrr ... I felt the Landcruiser move forward. This time, it wasn't sinking through the dry surface of the lake. Instead it moved forward slowly.

Then someone shouted, "Hey, it's working. The plane's wheels are up on the skids."

Ever so slowly, we moved forward, all ten of us busy with our assigned task. Either piloting a plane or a Landcruiser. Or moving skids or driftwood from rear to front.

Twice we had to interrupt our forward progress. Seems that, under the weight of the Landcruiser, some of the driftwood was breaking up and becoming buried in the sand. So a half dozen of us walked up the hill to gather an armload of replacement driftwood.

We rebuilt the driftwood tracks in front of the Landcruiser and returned to towing the plane. And sure enough, driving the Landcruiser, I finally arrived at the dirt road. I made a gradual left turn up and onto the road while wondering if the plane could make it up behind me. And I wondered too if the plane would be able to take off from a dirt road considerably more narrow and more bumpy than a dirt airstrip.

Revving his engines yet more, Dan was able to steer the plane up and onto the dirt road. We had done it! It took us four hours, but our team of ten had successfully towed the plane out of the lake and up onto the dirt road.

Dan climbed down from the plane to thank us and to say goodbye. We all smiled and hugged and congratulated each other. Then Dan and the girls climbed aboard the plane. The girls, especially, gave us an enthusiastic wave.

Then, revving his engines, Dan began a bouncy run down the dirt road and lifted off the ground. He gained just a bit of altitude when he turned to fly back toward us. He tipped his wings. I interpreted this as his official thank you.

I turned to Jim and asked, "Do you think we'll meet up with Dan in La Paz?"

Looking especially tired, Jim replied, "I hope not." ➤

Chapter 15

The Place Where Nobody Goes

I **FIRST LEARNED ABOUT TOROWEAP POINT** in September of 1969. That
month, *Desert* magazine published a special issue commemorating the
100th anniversary of Major John Wesley Powell's exploration of the Grand
Canyon. Powell was the first non-Native American to fully explore the
canyon. He and his party did so by navigating the Colorado River in four
wood boats. This was no small trick, considering the ferocity of the river's
rock-filled rapids. Though his exploration lasted a number of months, it's
officially dated September 1869.

While traveling the Colorado River, Powell became curious about a
particular place on the canyon's north rim where lava had flowed down to
the river from a volcanic cone now known as Vulcan's Throne. Believing
the volcano to be sacred, Powell's Indian guides refused to accompany him
on his climb up the lava spill onto the canyon's north rim. So Powell, along
with a few of his fellow explorers, climbed without the assistance of their
guides. This climb, by the way, was especially challenging for Powell, as
seven years earlier he lost an arm in the Civil War's Battle of Shiloh.

Powell and his party did make it up to the top of the rim. And in
arriving at the top, they discovered a spot on the canyon's rim where the

drop is a sheer vertical cliff, some three thousand feet straight down to the Colorado River. This place came to be known as Toroweap Point.

Among the articles in the September 1969 issue of *Desert* magazine was one titled, "The Place Where Nobody Goes." As suggested by the title of that article, Toroweap Point was a place not often visited, because back in the 1960s it was outside of the Grand Canyon National Park. Its designation, then, was Grand Canyon National *Monument.* Lacking park status, it came to the attention of relatively few. Also, its location on the canyon's more remote north rim, rather than the far more visited south rim, made it less accessible, thus far less visited.

Also, Toroweap Point was especially tough to get to. Sixty-three miles of dirt road passable in dry weather only. And when you got there, you'd find only two campsites in a clearing near the rim. Those campsites were complete with picnic table, fire ring, and outhouse. But no water. Clearly, this was a place for the more adventurous.

The article also mentioned retired mules. Those mules, which had spent their working life hauling visitors into and out of the canyon from the Park's south rim, were retired to Toroweap Point. There, they spent their remaining days grazing peacefully

The article also told of John Riffy, the ranger who lived at Toroweap Point. Seems that he had been stationed there for his entire career as a ranger—nearly all of his adult life. By the time I finished reading the article, "The Place Where Nobody Goes," I was eager to visit Toroweap Point.

I wanted to retrace the steps of John Wesley Powell. With one important difference: Having traveled by boat along the river, Powell had climbed from bottom to top and then back down. Arriving by car, I'd climb from top to bottom and then back up. So I wrote to Ranger Riffy asking about the trail down the lava spill to the river.

Within ten days or so, I received a letter from the ranger. He wrote, "There really isn't a trail. Just a series of rock monuments to mark the way."

I wrote back and told him that I'd be there the following spring. And that I'd find my way to the bottom.

Jim Hammond, my roommate, and Paul Griffith, a fellow I worked with, were both ready for adventure. The following May, we headed to Arizona in Jim's very old, very yellow, more dependable than pretty, Ford pickup truck. From Saint George, Utah, we turned south onto a reasonably smooth dirt road which we found on our auto club map. After a few miles, we slowed way down because the road became rough—rocks and potholes mainly. Before too long, we slowed down even more, this time to admire the scenery. The flat desert had given way to a series of small canyons among open ranch country. Cowboys on horseback were driving cattle through a dry creek, back toward their ranch.

In about another ten miles, the country flattened out again. I mentioned to Jim and Paul, "With the country this flat, I wonder how we'll know when we're coming upon the Grand Canyon."

Through a broad smile, Paul offered, "We'll see a sign that says 'Steep Downgrade Next 12 Feet.'"

All three of us laughed at his clever remark. Paul seemed delighted that his bit of humor was so well received.

About two miles before the canyon's rim, we saw a stone house to our left. And to our right, what looked like dirt runway. Also to our right was a makeshift wooden hanger that housed a small airplane. As Jim was a private pilot, he immediately recognized the plane as a Piper Cub.

I remembered reading in the article, "The Place Where Nobody Goes," that Ranger Riffy was a pilot. And he'd occasionally fly his plane up to Saint George to pick up mail and supplies. And to visit with friends.

Looking toward the stone house, we saw a man step out through the front door. We drove toward the house for our first look at John Riffy. He was tall, perhaps six feet plus an inch or two. And he was lanky. He wore beige cotton slacks and shirt. And a white cowboy hat.

From his stance, I could see that he was a man who was comfortable with himself. He offered us a friendly smile as we stepped down from the truck. Before he spoke even one word, I liked John Riffy.

Ranger Riffy and I began to speak about the same time. I explained that I was the fellow who'd written to him the previous September. He welcomed us to Toroweap Point and gave us the layout of the area. "There's no one else around so you'll have the whole place to yourselves. You can camp at either of the two campsites down by the rim."

I said, "We plan to climb down the lava spill in the morning. Where would we start our descent?"

He waved his arm toward the southwest, "Over there in that notch on the far side of the volcano. Just follow the road past the airport." Then he added, "Now you boys should hurry along to make camp and eat your supper before it gets dark."

As we drove toward the canyon rim to set up camp, I remembered something I'd read in the article, "The Place Where Nobody Goes." John Riffy lived alone in the stone house. At least he lived alone most of the time. He was married, but his wife was a college professor at the University of Washington in Seattle. She'd come down to stay with him during her vacations—Christmas, Easter, summer, and so forth. To me, this seemed a strange arrangement, but I guess it was OK with the ranger and Professor Riffy.

We drove over to the rim to set up camp. Stepping out onto a huge red boulder, we looked down in front of our toes to the Colorado River some three thousand feet below. As I looked across the canyon to the south, I remembered something that Ranger Riffy had told us. He said that to drive around to the south rim, just a fourth mile away as the crow flies, would require driving nearly 250 miles.

Off to the west, under the setting sun, we saw the lava spill leading down to the river. It looked to be about a 45-degree slope. That would make for a pretty steep hike over rough lava rock. But at least the hike would be short. A three-thousand-foot elevation change at 45 degrees would be just about a mile. Plus some extra distance for having to switch back and forth somewhat. For surely we wouldn't be able to descend in a straight line.

Ranger Riffy had told me, in his letter, that we likely wouldn't need a climbing rope. There was just one tough spot where we'd need to climb a small rock wall. But we planned to carry a small rope just in case. We would start right after breakfast the next morning. For now, we'd set up camp, have dinner, and get some sleep.

The next morning, we awoke with the sun, ate breakfast, and packed our backpacks. To get up to the head of the trail, we'd have to drive back through the meadow past Ranger Riffy's house and past the airstrip. Jim was very much looking forward to seeing the Piper Cub up close. In fact, he drove with his camera in his lap.

Approaching Ranger Riffy's house, we spotted him out by the tool shed.

"Good morning, Ranger Riffy."

"Morning, boys. Are you headed over to start your hike to the bottom?"

"Yes," I answered. "And we'll be spending the night down at the river. Would it be OK for us to leave our truck over in the notch?"

"Sure, that's fine." he said. And he added, "Later on, Buttercup and I will go up to check on you from the air."

It seemed to me that Buttercup was such a fine, gentle name for an airplane. I figured it must have been a smooth flying aircraft. When I asked Jim about it later, he told me that Piper Cubs are extremely smooth. "A real pleasure to fly," he promised.

So off we drove across the meadow, by the airport on our way to the notch on the far side of the volcano. As we approached the airport, we noted a wooden sign, which read, "Tuweep International Airport." A bit of

Ranger Riffy's humor. Tuweep, by the way, is the name of a yucca plant that is plentiful in this valley of the same name.

The hike down the lava spill took just a few hours. The rock monuments, piles of lava rock marking the way, were difficult to spot. For identically looking lava rock was lying about all over the place. But we found our way just fine. And the climb down wasn't especially dangerous or difficult. We even managed to climb down the small rock wall without using our rope.

We arrived at the river about a hundred yards upstream from the Lava Falls Rapids, one of the canyon's largest. We dropped our packs, rested for a bit, and drank some cool water from the river. It turned out that drinking water from the river was a bit of a trick. For the turbulence of the river mixed the water with a red-brown mud. This required that we scoop river water into a pan, let it settle for a while, then drink from the top of the pan. Thus we avoided the fourth of an inch of mud that settled at the bottom of the pan.

We walked downstream to have a look at the rapids. With each step, the intense roar grew louder. Arriving at the rapids, we were unable to communicate, even by shouting. It was simply impossible to hear anything but the roar of the water. The violent water seemed to be boiling, falling, and exploding, all at the same time. The enormous rapids filled the entire width of the river, perhaps forty yards or so.

After marveling at the rapids for about an hour, we hiked back upstream to where we had left our packs. By now it was midday and quite hot. Perhaps a hundred degrees. So we decided to go for a swim. And since we were above the rapids, we avoided the dangerous current by simply dunking our bodies into the water right along the shore. Since we'd brought along a climbing rope, one at a time we could venture farther out into the river while tied to the rope for protection. I secured one end of the rope around a boulder on shore, took off all of my clothes, then tied the other end of the rope around my waist. I then swam out into the river to test the protection system.

Not only did it work just fine, but also it was really a lot of fun. I swam out perpendicular to the shore for ten or fifteen yards or so, then the current caught me and swung me downstream with considerable force. Thanks to the rope tied around my waist, I simply swung back toward the shore one rope length downstream. Kind of like a large wet pendulum. Just one problem, the water was icy cold. So between swims, I came out of the water and sat on the shore for a while to warm up. I occupied myself with this swimming, swinging, warming up cycle for about a half hour.

The air was growing still hotter. Jim, who was not inclined to swim in the cold water, sat in shallow water at the shore. From time to time, he'd splash some water on his head, shoulders, and back. Paul, even less inclined to enter the cold water, was looking for an alternative way to cool off. And he found it.

Seems he'd found a cave in the rock wall about thirty yards upstream. He called on us to join him, so Jim and I put on our shorts and walked up to the cave. The entrance to the cave was about eight feet wide and three feet high. So we crawled in on our hands and knees. It was quite a bit cooler inside, so the three of us crawled in about twenty feet or so and lay down. We relaxed in the cave for about an hour. Just idling away the afternoon talking about this and that. Until we heard a woman's voice.

All three of us went scampering out from our comfortable cave into the glaring sunlight. "Where in the world is that woman's voice coming from?" asked Paul.

We immediately had our answer. Out in the middle of the river, a small raft floated with the current. "Wow, it's a raft approaching the rapids!" shouted Jim. "Looks like three people aboard."

If the raft were going over the rapids, we'd want to witness the event. So we began walking downstream at a quick pace.

But we really didn't need to hurry. As we later learned, rafters would customarily pull up on the beach just above each large rapids. They'd then walk over to survey the rapids and plan their approach. So the raft put up on the far shore directly across from us. Three people, all wearing bathing suits and life preservers. Two men and one woman. They saw us and gave us a wave. We waved back.

They walked downstream to the rapids. We walked along with them on our side of the river. We watched as they pointed to various sections of the rapids. They discussed the situation for about twenty minutes before returning to their raft.

They pushed off from the beach and paddled out into the middle of the river. Their raft caught the current and turned downstream. All three of them paddled furiously, seemingly trying to enter the rapids in some predetermined spot. As the raft approached the rapids, it moved along more and more quickly. And it began to bob up and down along the surface of the turbulent water. All three passengers stopped paddling and grabbed onto the lifeline strung along both sides of the raft. Then, right out in the middle of the rapids, the raft disappeared, falling into a hole in the water.

Paul, who had done some river rafting, explained that just below any powerful rapids, was a deep depression in the surface of the water. I remember counting, "one, two, three ..." It seemed to me that the raft was gone from sight for about four seconds. Finally, the raft and its rope-holding rafters came shooting out from the downstream end of the hole. And as it shot up out of the hole, it flew up into the air. How high? Oh maybe seven or eight feet. While it was impossible to hear anything other than the roar of the water, I was sure that all three of the rafters were screaming. For each of them had their mouth wide open.

When the raft landed back on the surface of the water, it was with considerable impact. I wondered what it felt like, sitting on the raft, having fallen from a height of perhaps seven or eight feet onto the surface of the water. Once it hit the water, the raft scooted along the turbulent surface, much as it did before entering the hole in the water. Still the passengers held onto the lifelines. Then, seemingly all together, they released their grip and took up their paddles. As the raft floated away from the bottom of the rapids, the turbulent water gave way to smooth. All aboard the raft stopped paddling and looked upstream toward the rapids they had just survived. They raised their paddles, apparently in celebration. Then they slowly drifted downstream and out of sight.

Jim, Paul, and I started back along the shore toward our comfortable cave. As it was then late afternoon, the air temperature had dropped somewhat. We also noted a cool breeze coming down the river. About the time we got far enough from the rapids that we could carry on a conversation, we heard an airplane. Looking up, we saw Buttercup. We waved and, in turn, the plane rolled first to the left, then to the right.

The sun dropped behind the canyon's south wall and the air temperature fell further. We spent a half hour or so sitting comfortably, staring at the river, and chatting about this and that. We cooked and ate dinner, then spread out our blankets on the beach. Lying beside the river, we watched the evening stars filling an ever-darkening sky.

Looking up at the night sky from the bottom of the Grand Canyon is a particularly splendid sight for a couple of reasons. First, the air is ever so clear, so the sky is ever so dark and the stars are ever so bright. Second, the sky is framed on both the north and the south by the rims of the canyon. So the star-filled sky appears as a broad irregular ribbon above. We lay there just staring at the sky and counting the shooting stars. Until the wind came up.

The strong, downstream wind, caused by differential temperatures along the floor of the canyon, blew fine sand along the beach. We struggled, unsuccessfully, to keep the sand from getting into our ears and nostrils. Then we remembered the cave.

I think it was Paul who suggested we sleep in the cave. I agreed that it was a great idea. So Paul and I grabbed our blankets and headed for the cave. Jim, for whatever reason, decided to stay on the beach and brave the wind.

Paul and I ducked down and entered the cave on our hands and knees. We crawled back about ten feet where we were out of the wind. This sleeping in the cave seemed an absolutely wonderful solution. We yelled over to Jim inviting him to join us in the cave, but he stayed on the beach.

Without the beautiful sky to hold our interest, both Paul and I began doze off. Then, suddenly, I was awakened by the sound of Paul screaming. Startled, I opened my eyes and saw Paul, blanket in hand, scurrying out from the mouth of the cave. He was accompanied by who knows how many bats, all flying around him. I grabbed my blanket and scurried out from the cave following quickly behind Paul and the bats.

The remainder of the night found all three of us down on the beach, rolled tightly in our blankets. We did our best, though we were generally unsuccessful, to keep the fine sand from getting into our ears and nostrils. The wind continued for perhaps another hour or so. After that, though already gritty with fine sand, we slept soundly.

The next morning, we awoke at first light. We had decided to start up out of the canyon early, thus avoiding the intense midday heat. We bathed in shallow water to remove the fine sand from our hair and body. We ate a quick, cold breakfast and packed up. Then we began the steep climb up the lava spill.

The climb up went fine. Again, we were able to negotiate the rock wall without using our rope. We arrived up on the rim in plenty of time for an early lunch.

We rested by the truck for a time, then drove over to Ranger Riffy's house to tell him we were back up top. He wasn't there. So we headed back to our camp by the edge of the rim. On the way, we ran into Ranger Riffy. We chatted with him for a while, then drove over to our camp at the rim. Jim, Paul, and I all looked forward to another beautiful, star-filled evening. And now that we were on top of the rim, the air temperature would be considerably more comfortable. And we wouldn't have to deal with blowing sand. Instead, we'd enjoy another jet-black sky filled with an infinite number of stars.

We weren't disappointed. The night sky was, once again, spectacular. And the wind, just about nonexistent. Perhaps it was blowing down along the river, but not up top. We sat outside our tent for hours, enjoying the sky and counting the shooting stars. It was that evening when we first talked about coming back the following year. And again hiking down to the bottom.

As we drove out the next morning, reluctantly leaving the place where nobody goes, we stopped to say goodbye to Range Riffy. And to tell him we'd be back again the following year.

"OK boys, I'll watch for you," he said with a smile and a wave of his hand. ➤

Chapter 16

Swimming Above the Rapids

JIM, PAUL, AND I RETURNED TO TOROWEAP POINT the following May. "Hello Ranger Riffy," we said as we stepped out of the truck.

"Hello boys, glad to see you again."

We chatted for a while, then he suggested we make camp and cook dinner before dark. So we drove out to the rim where we, once again, had the campground all to ourselves. We ate dinner and sat around the campfire enjoying the rapidly cooling air and a gentle breeze.

Before too long, we heard a truck approaching. It was John Riffy driving out to visit. He stopped his truck, turned off the engine and walked over to join us at the campfire. "Would you like a cup of coffee?" Paul asked.

"Yes, thank you," replied John Riffy.

Sipping coffee, Ranger Riffy told us about a government surveyor who had recently contacted him about coming by to survey the area. "He's specifically interested in the topography around the volcano, Vulcan's Throne. The surveyor mentioned that he might do the climb down to the bottom. Very likely, he'll show up during the next day or so. And seeing as how you boys have recent experience climbing down and back up, perhaps you might offer the fellow some useful information."

"We'll be happy to offer any help that we can," said Jim. "In fact, if he shows up by early tomorrow morning, we'll be glad to show him the way down to the river."

Ranger Riffy said, "Thanks boys." He spent perhaps another half hour visiting with us by the campfire. Then he bid goodnight, got into his truck, and drove back to his house.

We slept well that night and woke just before sunrise. Following breakfast, we piled our packs into the truck and drove toward the notch adjacent to Vulcan's Throne. From there, as before, we'd begin our hike down the lava spill to the river. As we passed by Ranger Riffy's house, we saw him standing out front. We waved and shouted, "Good morning."

He waved back and shouted, "I'll fly over with Buttercup later in the day." We, of course, expected him to say exactly that. In fact, if he hadn't said so, we'd expect him to fly over anyway.

The climb down to the river felt different this second time. The wondering and anticipating about an unknown route had preoccupied our minds the year before. This time, we had no such preoccupation. As we'd previously made the decent, we weren't wondering if we could make it. We knew we could. It was just a matter of remembering the route. As it turned out, we remembered the route quite well. And we arrived at the bottom in good time and without incident.

Again it was hot at the bottom. And again, we decided on a swim to cool off. More willing to brave the cold water this year than last, Jim and Paul took turns tying into the rope to protect themselves from the strong current. I suppose it was the heat that made me eager to get into the water. So I decided to walk upstream a bit and from there swim across the river. I figured that if I were to go upstream far enough, I'd be a safe distance above the rapids. Since I was a pretty strong swimmer, I was sure I'd make it.

So wearing not a stitch of clothes, I hiked upstream about seventy yards. I walked out onto a sandbar, dove into the cold water, and began swimming to the far shore. Although I was quite chilled, swimming the first ten yards or so went fine. Then the current caught me. I knew that the current would carry me downstream a bit. But once caught by the current, I was surprised by how strong it was. Then, just about in the middle of the river, I became less confident in my ability to make it to the far shore before entering the rapids.

Out in the middle of the river, with the current pulling me toward the rapids, I had to swim with all of my strength. Swimming toward the far shore just as hard as I could, I suddenly felt a sharp pain in both of my calves. Exertion from swimming, combined with the very cold water, had caused both of my legs to cramp. The intense pain convinced me that my legs would be of no help in swimming. So I swam with my arms only while dragging my stiff legs behind me through the cold water.

I had already drifted downstream as far as I'd earlier hiked upstream. To add terror to my pain, I could hear the roar of the rapids growing louder. The louder that roar, the more I feared being dashed against some large rock. That thought inspired me to swim yet harder. And so I did. At least I think I did. I'm really not sure. The pain in my legs was horrible, but I had to ignore the pain and continue to swim, arms only, just as hard as I could.

Finally, I found some encouragement when I felt the current diminish. I had gotten close enough to the far shore that the current there was less strong. Though ever so encouraged, I was still fearful of the rapids. So I continued to stroke forcefully. Soon I began to see that though very close to the rapids, I'd likely make it safely across the river.

I felt the sandy bottom of the river, first in my fingers. Then on my knees and my toes. I was in eighteen or twenty inches of water at the shore. I crawled up almost onto the beach and paused to catch my breath. My face landed in dry sand while my body remained in a few inches of water. Using perhaps my last bit of strength, I dragged my body up a few more feet onto the beach. So the backs of my legs were out of the water. And there, safe at last on the far shore, I fell into a deep sleep.

When I awoke, perhaps an hour later, I felt groggy. And hot. The temperature down along the river was probably one hundred degrees. My face was covered in fine sand, and my back, my bottom, and the backs of my legs were sunburned. In fact, quite sunburned. In the safety of shallow water, I bathed both to cool off and to remove the sand from my body.

Across the river, I saw Paul and Jim. Paul waved. I waved back. It then occurred to me that Paul and Jim likely had no idea that I had been in danger while swimming across the river. They probably figured that all was OK and that I swam over without incident. Man, did I have a story for them!

The only way back, of course, was to swim across the river again. But this time, I'd be more careful. For one, I'd hike farther upstream than the seventy yards I hiked earlier. Also, I'd make sure to swim from a sandbar on one side to a sandbar on the other. That way, I'd minimize the distance I'd have to swim. And I'd bathe in the river for a time before starting to swim. That way, I'd acclimatize my muscles to the cold water.

I hiked up river about one hundred yards and walked out onto a sandbar and sat for a time in the cold water. I rubbed my calves under water. My legs still hurt. And my arm and shoulder muscles were sore.

Ten minutes later, I began swimming back across the river. Again the current caught me, but I had hiked far enough upstream that I was making good progress. I actually drifted somewhat farther downstream than I had anticipated. Once again, I had underestimated the current. No matter though, I soon came upon another sandbar a bit further downstream. I had made it across. Though my calf, shoulder, and arm muscles were sore, and the entire back of my body was sunburned, I was no longer in danger.

I spent the next fifteen minutes telling Jim and Paul about my earlier swim across the river. As I had thought, they had no idea that I had been in danger. Seems they had simply been lounging around on the shore, and they too fell asleep for a while.

Then we heard a familiar sound. Buttercup first dipped her left wing and then her right. All three of us stood up and waved enthusiastically. Paul and Jim with their clothes on.

The afternoon had been uncomfortably hot. So we were glad when the sun finally fell behind the south rim. That evening, as a million stars appeared in an ever-darkening sky, we lay on the sand and talked about the wonders of nature. We also discussed our climb back up the next morning and agreed to get started early.

Unlike our windy night at the river a year earlier, this time there was only a gentle breeze. Paul and Jim both slept well. I not so well. For my muscles ached and my sunburn did too. Maybe I got three or four hours sleep in a series of thirty-minute naps.

We started early the next morning and climbed up to the top without incident. Halfway up, we first heard, and then saw, Buttercup above. She first dipped her left wing and then her right. We waved. She flew away.

When we got back up to the truck, Jim reached for a cold drink in the ice chest. "Hey, you guys want a Coke?" he asked.

"No thanks, Jim," I replied. "And I wouldn't have a cold drink just yet. We're far too hot. I'd cool off for a while before putting a cold drink on my stomach."

Apparently, Jim had been very much looking forward to an ice cold drink. And my warning wasn't about to dissuade him from having one. So he popped open a can of Coke and quickly gulped it down.

Within just a few minutes, Jim was complaining of stomach cramps. And then he threw up. And then he reached into his pack and dug out a roll of toilet paper, and walked off to find some privacy. When he returned, Paul and I were lying in the shade of the truck, sipping warm water from our water bottle. The three of us rested in the shade of the truck for perhaps another half hour.

As we drove back toward Ranger Riffy's house, we spotted a green pickup truck. Coming closer, we saw a man step out from the driver's side of the truck. As we pulled up beside the truck, we read the emblem on the door, "U.S. Geological Survey."

"Hey," said Paul, "I'll bet this is the surveyor John Riffy told us about. Maybe he'll have some questions about the route down the lava spill to the bottom."

"Hi, fellas," the man offered.

"Hi."

"The ranger tells me that you've been to the bottom. So you know the route and that you could tell me about it."

"Yeah, we went down yesterday, camped at the bottom and just came up about an hour ago."

"I've got to go down tomorrow," he offered. "And I'm not looking forward to it at all. Today I'm making some measurements up here on top, but tomorrow I'll go down to make some measurements by the river. I've heard it's a very difficult climb. Is that so?"

It was obvious that this fellow was afraid of climbing down to the bottom. And It seemed to occur to Jim, Paul, and me, all at the same time, that we might "lay it on thick." And so we did. Since we had done the climb twice, we knew that it wasn't all that difficult. But we weren't about to say so to this government fellow. So I told him, "The climb is absolutely dreadful!"

Paul said, "It's really dangerous. There's sharp lava rock all over the place. And it's super easy to fall and get cut up badly."

Jim added, "The trail is very narrow and it follows along the top of a high cliff. And, this time of year, the heat is intense."

I added, "Each of us experienced a dizzy sensation, especially on the climb back up."

Jim said, "We'd never consider going back down there again."

You're not going to carry much weight in your pack, are you?" I asked.

"Oh, my instruments weigh about thirty-five pounds," he replied.

"Wow, I'm sure glad we didn't have to carry that kind of weight. That would, make the climb up far more difficult," I suggested.

Jim asked, "You'll stay down there overnight, won't you?"

"No," he replied. "I'll go down and back up tomorrow."

"Oh my gosh!" said Jim. "We've never gone both down and back up in the same day. In fact, I don't think I've ever heard of anyone doing that."

"Well, good luck, hope you make it," Paul offered. Then we drove away.

We held back our laughter until we had driven about a hundred yards and then, all at once, we laughed out loud. I laughed so hard that, just for a moment, I forgot about my sunburn. Paul said, "We probably caused that government fellow to lose a night's sleep worrying about his climb tomorrow."

We drove over to Ranger Riffy's house.

"How'd it go, boys?" he asked.

"Fine, Ranger Riffy. But we're hot and tired. We're looking forward to relaxing in camp."

"Good," he said. "You boys go on down to camp. I'll drive over after dark and visit with you."

We drove to our camp by the rim. Instead of busying ourselves about dinner, we simply sat on the edge of the rim with our feet dangling in space. We looked down, between our boots, at the Colorado River some three thousand feet below. Though we were very tired, it was a pleasant kind of tired. Like the physical tired that comes from having done something of significance.

The sky darkened and the air turned cool. The wind picked up just a bit. The stars appeared in an indigo blue sky, and it occurred to me that it was really quite wonderful to be alive.

It was hunger that finally drove us the thirty yards back from the edge of the rim to camp. We enjoyed a late dinner by the light of our lantern. And just as we finished cleaning up, we heard Ranger Riffy's truck approaching.

"Want some coffee, Ranger Riffy," offered Paul.

"Sure," answered Ranger Riffy.

Sitting around the campfire, we confessed to Ranger Riffy that we had "laid it on thick" for the government surveyor. I'm really not sure if we were confessing or if we were boasting, but we took it as forgiveness that Ranger Riffy chuckled at our story. I don't remember how long we sat around the campfire that evening, staring into the flames. Feeling the cool air swirling around our heads and shoulders. Occasionally looking up at the clear, dark sky filled with a million stars. All I can tell you is that I wanted that evening never to end.

Jim, Paul, and I all slept well that night. Early the next morning, we packed up to leave, then drove up to Ranger Riffy's house to say goodbye.

"We'll be back next year," we told him.

"OK, boys. I'll be looking forward to seeing you then."

As we drove north along sixty-three miles of bumpy dirt road, it occurred to me that Toroweap Point had become something special to us. In a way, it had become kind of "our place." And we thought of John Riffy, not so much as a ranger in a national monument, but rather as our friend. ➤

Chapter 17

Horse Thief Canyon

J IM, PAUL, AND I RETURNED to Toroweap Point another two or three times. For a few years in a row, it was our annual event. Each time we said goodbye to John Riffy, we assured him we'd be back. And each time we kept our word.

Strange thing though, the last time the three of us were there together, we noted that this old-as-the-hills place was changing rapidly. The first time we went to the bottom in May of 1970 we saw just one small raft running the rapids. But on each return, we saw an ever-increasing number. And with that ever-increasing number of rafts, the river felt less and less like a wilderness.

The final time we went to the bottom, in May of 1973 or maybe 1974, it wasn't a wilderness at all. A film crew was shooting a movie at the top of Lava Flow Rapids. There must have been twenty or more people milling around on the far shore. They were struggling to position cameras along the beach and on the rocks near the rapids. They had two large rafts on the shore, but none in the water.

And there were helicopters. Two of them. They were ferrying people and equipment from who knows where to a sandbar above the falls. Because of the roar of the rapids, we couldn't hear the sounds of their activities. Except, of course, when a helicopter took off or landed. Then, the blowing sand was accompanied by the whir of the helicopter's engine.

The film crew worked until late afternoon when the helicopters then began shuttling the whole menagerie off to wherever they had come from. We figured perhaps Saint George, Utah, the closest city. Or maybe Las Vegas. When the last helicopter took off with its load of people and stuff, we were alone at the bottom as in years past. We sat quietly for a while, I, for one, feeling sad. We figured that the film crew would return sometime the next morning. Not wanting to see them again, we decided to climb back up at sunrise.

That evening was pleasant. Dark sky, lots of stars and a gentle breeze. None of us said so out loud, but I think we all knew that this would be our last trip to the bottom.

Jim, Paul, and I had always done this trip in the month of May. So I became curious about visiting Toroweap Point during other times of the year. On a trip to Southern Utah during the month of February, Ben Richardson and I tried to include a visit to Toroweap Point. But we couldn't make it. The dirt road leading into the monument was slick with mud. As we were traveling in Ben's two-wheel drive sedan, we had hardly the vehicle to negotiate sixty-three miles of red-brown ooze.

Ben and I finally made it to Toroweap Point the following winter. In fact, we negotiated the road easily. Not only did we have benefit of my four-wheel drive Toyota Landcruiser, we also drove on frozen, near solid ground. We didn't climb to the bottom during that trip, but instead hiked around at the top of the rim. Ben was interested in both photography and geology, so we spent our time taking photographs and looking at rocks through a magnifying glass.

We hadn't told John Riffy that we'd be coming, so he was surprised to see us. No doubt he'd gotten used to seeing me drive up, with Jim and Paul, in Jim's yellow truck during the month of May. But there we were, Ben and I, in the dead of winter. Ranger Riffy smiled when we drove up and he welcomed us as usual.

After visiting with John Riffy just briefly, we drove down to the campground near the rim. As the winter day was short, we hurried to set up camp. That night, the temperature dropped to fifteen degrees under a clear sky. Having brought along our warmest sleeping bags, both Ben and I slept comfortably.

The following morning, Ben crawled out of the tent early. He set up his camera on a tripod right at the edge of the rim. From there, he captured some memorable photos. Then we cooked a hot breakfast and spent most of the morning hiking around looking for fossils. We hiked east from camp about a mile or so and noticed, off in the distance, the land falling away into a canyon leading down to the river. I then began to think about the possibility of doing a climb down to the river in that canyon. I mentioned this idea to Ben. He told me, in no uncertain terms, that he wasn't interested in "anything that aggressive."

That afternoon, I asked John Riffy if he knew of a route down to the river in the canyon that I had spotted. He told me, "Yes, there is a route down Horse Thief Canyon about seven miles east. But it isn't easy. It requires a climbing rope in one place. And the place where you descend by rope, you probably wouldn't be able to climb back up. So you'd have to make your way down the river, back to the lava spill at Vulcan's Throne. There, you could climb back up on the route you already know."

"What would be the best time of year to make that trip?" I asked.

"Oh, in the late fall, I'd say. That's when the river is lowest. You'd have to hike about seven miles downriver, and you'd do that most easily, and most safely, in low water." Then he added, "Don't underestimate the ruggedness of the country to the east along the rim. It's rough. In fact, back in the 1940s, two head of cattle got loose from a ranch just to the north of here. They actually made their way along the rim to the east. Two cowboys from the ranch, out on horseback, tracked the cattle and followed them along the rim. But the country was so rugged they couldn't drive the cattle back out. So they slaughtered them right there, built a fire, and cooked them to jerky. Took 'em three days."

John Riffy was saying the exact words I wanted to hear. He was telling me that the trip would be an absolutely wonderful adventure. An expedition. So I told him I'd plan the trip and find an adventurous friend to do it with me.

Rich Goedl decided the trip would be fun. He and I had done some backpacking together in the California Sierras. "Sure, let's do the trip, how about next Thanksgiving?" suggested Rich. "How much time do you think we'll need?"

"About five days for the hike, I figure. So with a day and a half drive each way, we can do it if we stretch the Thanksgiving weekend into eight days. Nine to be really safe."

On the topographic map, we clearly saw the contours of Horse Thief Canyon. It really was rough! We'd have to be careful. An accident in such a remote place and we'd wait a day or more before help could arrive.

The following November, Rich and I drove to the monument in crisp, clear weather. "Hello, Ranger Riffy," I said. "This is my friend, Rich Goedl. We've come to do the trip down Horse Thief Canyon."

"Hi, boys. And welcome. Will you be setting up camp at the rim tonight?"

"Yes," I answered. "But we'll start our hike first thing in the morning, so we'll pack up and abandon camp then. Where can we leave the Landcruiser when we start hiking?"

"Oh, just drive out about a quarter of a mile east to where the jeep trail ends. Your truck won't be in anyone's way. In fact, we're unlikely to see anyone else here this time of year."

126

"OK, we'll drive out there first thing in the morning, then begin hiking."

And just as I expected, Ranger Riffy said, "I'll fly over to check on you boys."

As we drove over to the rim to set up camp, I wondered if John Riffy regularly flew over to check up on us out of concern for our safety. Or did he simply like to fly? Maybe our hiking around the monument offered him the excuse to get up in the air. While I wasn't sure of the reason, I was glad he did check up on us because it added a margin of safety to our outings. And it also felt good to think we might be adding to his enjoyment. Especially since he lived alone in such a remote place.

After dinner, Rich and I went to sleep early, in part because we wanted to get a good night's sleep before our early morning start. And also because, that late in the season, the sun set early and the temperature dropped quickly.

It was still dark when we awoke the next morning. We lay in our sleeping bags until first light appeared, then emerged to gobble down a quick breakfast. Well before the day warmed noticeably, we were on our way. We drove out to where Ranger Riffy had told us to leave the Landcruiser and put on our backpacks.

Our packs were necessarily heavy. In addition to the usual tent, sleeping bag, food, and clothing, we also carried a 150-foot climbing rope, a few carabineers, and some nylon climbing slings. We weren't sure just how difficult the wall in the canyon might be and we wanted to be prepared.

We also carried a three-day supply of water. We figured we'd need a day to hike along the rim to the head of Horse Thief Canyon, then a day down to the river. There, we'd have all the water we needed for the rest of our trip. We carried one extra day's supply of water, just in case.

But it wasn't the weight of our packs that caused us to move so slowly. It was the ruggedness of the terrain. We quickly realized that to hike from one point to another along the rim, traveling in a straight line was impossible.

There was always another rocky ridge or a pile of large boulders to walk around. And rocks to step over. And cacti to avoid. And dozens of minor canyons, first to descend, then walk back up some fifty yards later. Our topographic map had contour markings of fifty feet intervals. But our obstacles included many thirty- to forty-foot depressions in the landscape. This hike along the rim was much harder than we had envisioned. As a result, our travel was much slower than we had expected.

By noon, when we stopped for a rest and some food, we were disappointed at how little progress we had made. We figured that we had traveled only a couple of miles along the rim. We had expected we'd cover more like seven miles that day, and we had already used up half of our daylight. At this rate, we'd need an extra day just to hike to the head of Horse Thief Canyon. Were we to require that extra day, we'd use up our reserve of water before we even entered the canyon. We'd done exactly what Ranger Riffy had warned us not to do. We had underestimated the ruggedness of the country. We decided to continue hiking until late afternoon. Then, if our progress didn't improve, we'd camp for the night and reevaluate our situation.

About mid-afternoon, I heard a familiar sound and looked up. Buttercup flew overhead. First she dipped her left wing, then her right. Rich and I waved. I wondered what Ranger Riffy was thinking. Had he expected us to have made more progress hiking these many hours? Or had he been so terribly sure of the ruggedness of the country that he knew we'd be doing no better than we were? Maybe I'd ask him this question when we next saw him.

The afternoon went just the same as the morning. Painfully slow traveling through terribly rugged country. Both very tired, we made camp in a flat spot surrounded by boulders. And while neither Rich nor I was quite ready to say so, we were both aware that we'd likely have to turn back in the morning.

Though concerned for the success of our expedition, we were actually having a wonderful time. Whether or not we'd ever see Horse Thief Canyon, we were hiking in one of the most rugged and beautiful places we'd ever visited.

In the morning, with rested bodies and clear heads, we evaluated our situation. We had hiked only three and a half to four miles. At this rate, we'd need another day just to complete the seven miles to the head of Horse Thief Canyon. Then, if all went well, we'd need one more day to descend the canyon to the river. We had carried along the three-day water supply in case we needed an extra day in the canyon. But now we found we'd need that extra day just to *get* to the canyon. Our safety factor was gone.

If only there had been recent rain. Then we would have found water puddles on some of the larger boulders. But it hadn't rained recently. According to our topographic map, there was a spring on top of the bluff to the north. But it was likely a good part of a day's hike there and back. That seemed too far out of our way. Such a significant detour, while offering water, would cost us time, energy, and food.

As sad as the decision was for us, we simply had to turn around and head back. With an early start, we'd be back at the Landcruiser before dark. And so, disappointed as we were, we began the slow hike west over the same rugged country we had hiked east upon the day before.

It was about mid-morning when Buttercup flew overhead. As usual, she first tipped her left wing and then her right. Also as usual, we waved back. Ranger Riffy then knew we had aborted our trip and were hiking out. It occurred to me that if he had been concerned for our safety, he was likely relieved that we were hiking out rather than descending Horse Thief Canyon.

It was late afternoon when we arrived back at the Landcruiser. Both Rich and I were tired and disappointed. We decided that before driving down to the rim to set up camp, we'd stop by to tell Range Riffy we'd made it back. And to explain that we moved so slowly that we had to abort the trip.

He listened to our story and, I'm sure, he clearly sensed our disappointment. And then he said something that took Rich and me by surprise. He said, "I'll bet you boys could use a steak dinner and a cold beer."

"Oh yes!" Rich and I replied in unison.

"OK, you boys go down to the rim and set up camp before it gets dark. Then come on back up to the house. I'll see you there."

All at once, Rich and I forgot our disappointment about aborting our trip. We also forgot about our tiredness. All we could think of, while setting up camp, was hurrying back to Ranger Riffy's house to join him for a steak and a cold beer. And, for me, it wasn't the steak dinner and beer that I was so looking forward to. It was more than that. Much more. It was that we were about to have dinner with John Riffy in his home.

As we sat at the dinner table enjoying steak cooked to order, salad, baked potato, and beer, we talked about all sorts of things. About what Rich and I did for a living, about our friends and our families and our interests. John Riffy told us about how much he loved Toroweap Point. And how it was to live by himself in such a remote place. And how he was able to fly up to Saint George when he needed supplies. And in Saint George, he had some friends with whom he'd occasionally visit. And that some of the ranchers from north in Tuweep Valley would stop by for a chat every once in a while. And that his wife came down to spend her school holidays with him at Toroweap Point. So he wasn't alone all of the time.

As he spoke, he affirmed what we already knew. That John Riffy simply loved this place where nobody goes. That because of his love for this land, he had dedicated his life to overseeing this spot, which was every bit as beautiful as it was rugged and remote.

"Rich, would you like another beer? asked Ranger Riffy.

"Yes, thank you. I would like another beer."

While sharing dinner with John Riffy that evening, it didn't occur to me that this would be the one and only time I'd ever be inside of his house. And when we drove away the next morning, and I promised to return as usual, it didn't occur to me that I'd never again see John Riffy.

About a decade went by. Then one September during the mid-1980s, my wife, two sons and I took a family vacation to the North Rim of The Grand Canyon National Park. Oh, I guess Larry was about six years old, and Doug about four. We stayed in a cabin and ate our meals in the lodge.

Though we hiked around mainly on our own, on one particular day, we attended a ranger-led nature walk. The ranger was an energetic young lady who lectured about the formation of the canyon and about the flora and fauna of the Kaibab Plateau where we were standing.

When someone asked her a question about the mules that carry passengers and supplies to the bottom, she offered that the mule trips go out from the south rim rather than the north. Then she told of a remote place to the west, a place where the mules are put out to retire. She didn't name Toroweap Point.

At the end of her talk, I asked if she'd been to Toroweap Point. She said, "No, but I've heard it's hard to get to."

"Do you know the ranger there?" I asked. "A fellow named John Riffy. He's been there his whole career."

"No," she answered. "I didn't know him. Though I've heard of him. Another ranger told me that he died about two years ago."

"Oh."

The boys and I stepped back away from the group. Then, a few minutes later, Doug asked, "Why are you crying, Daddy." ➤

Part Four

Thinking and Feeling

AS I APPROACHED MIDDLE AGE, my life changed—a whole bunch. I had married my first wife when I was thirty-six. Larry, my first son, was born when I was thirty-eight. Also at age thirty-eight, I obtained my MBA degree and launched my management consulting practice. When I was forty, my son Doug was born.

I'm sure it was the combination of these significant life changes that made me more introspective. I found myself reflecting on values. And on lessons learned. In fact, I made an especially interesting discovery. I discovered that adventure can be other than physical. It can also be intellectual. Or emotional.

Chapter 18

What Mountains Mean to Me

IN **NOVEMBER OF 1964,** I visited The Grand Canyon National Park for the first time. Hiking down to the bottom, I stopped at the Bright Angel Campground for a drink of water and a brief rest in the shade. There, I met a small, energetic fellow from Brooklyn, New York. He said that he worked in a photo darkroom and that, once or twice a year, he traveled west to hike in the mountains or canyons of the western United States. "To experience the energy!" he announced with great emphasis. He spent the next twenty minutes telling me how hiking in the wilderness charged his emotional batteries.

Since he was hiking uphill and I down, we soon parted. I walked along the trail thinking, *Emotional batteries! What's he talking about? I think the guy's a wacko. Maybe he's been alone in the darkroom too long. For he's entirely too emotional about mountains.*

But as the years marched by, and as I thought about my own wilderness experiences, I found myself becoming more and more aligned with his emotional feeling about mountains and canyons. In fact, I think, over time, I changed from climbing on a physical level to climbing on an emotional level. Yes, I'll explain.

You see, I think that if a person sets out to climb a mountain, he can do so on one of three different levels. First, he can climb on a physical level. Here, the climber thinks mainly about arriving at the summit and getting back down safely. Considerations in his mind include physical conditioning, proper equipment, food, water, weather conditions, and time.

If you speak with him about hiking or climbing, he'll tell you that an average person on an average day's hike, carrying an average sized backpack will burn about a pound of fat—approximately thirty-five hundred calories. And that a hiker should allow about an hour for each two to three miles on the trail plus an additional hour for every thousand feet of elevation gain.

But the person who climbs solely for the physical experience won't really have a full appreciation of the mountain. Not choosing to examine a lodgepole pine, or stare into a babbling brook, he'll move along as fast as his muscles and lungs permit. He may, or may not, invite others along for company. And he might not return to climb the same mountain for a second time. Because many who climb on a physical level feel compelled to count the mountains they've conquered.

The second level of climbing a mountain is intellectual. Here, the climber has a greater appreciation for his surroundings. He may recognize that a particular mountain is formed from granite and has been uplifted to the west by earthquakes. Or he may know to look for the single needle pinion pine on the dryer eastern side of the mountain. This climber's library will include books on ecology. And he may well carry a camera.

Finally, one can climb a mountain on an emotional level. For those who do so, moving upon the mountain is more important than arriving at its summit. For here the important thing is the doing. Walking on the mountain, surrounded by both its silence and its sounds. Gliding along its contours. Touching its rocks. Many, like the small, energetic fellow I met in the Grand Canyon, would describe this as a spiritual experience.

For those who climb on an emotional level, it's OK to be alone. For when alone, one can move at his or her own pace. Slowly perhaps. Taking the time to savor the smell of a damp meadow, the quiet of a high mountain lake, and the coldness of granite in the shade.

One who climbs on an emotional level will likely return to the same mountain more than once. In fact, he'll have his favorites. And he'll tell you about his favorite sections on his favorite climbs: The deep cut to the left of the snow patch there in the shade. The cool meadow just beyond the upper pine rimmed lake. The marvelous panoramic view from the upper shelf just above the steep switchback.

For many years, I thought that climbing was simply a physical experience. That's when I learned about calories, lightweight tents, and predicting how long it might take to climb a particular peak. When I met the "wacko" in the Grand Canyon, I wasn't ready to hear what he was telling me. He was speaking on an emotional level and I was capable of listening only on a physical level. Clearly we weren't communicating.

Later, as I gained experience in the mountains, I moved on to the intellectual level. My library grew to include books about ecology. My collection of photographs also grew. And my pace slowed significantly.

It took quite a number of years, but eventually, I discovered that simply being on the mountain gifted me with a special feeling. A particular emotion that I experience nowhere else. And I returned, again and again, to climb my favorites, like Mount Winchell in the Sierras and Mopah Peak in the desert. And, at long last, I came to understand the fellow I had met in the Grand Canyon so many years earlier.

The Trinity Alps

In the summer of 1975, I camped for a few days in Northern California's Trinity Alps. The Trinity Alps aren't massive and rugged like the Sierra Nevada range. Instead they're gentle and rolling.

From the campground, I hiked alone to a small lake where I hoped to catch some trout. Along the trail, I saw only two other people: a man and a woman coming down from the lake. After seeing that one couple, I was alone for the rest of the day. My hike was so very peaceful. And quiet. Just the sounds of the squirrels and the birds. And the wind blowing through the trees. And the crunch, crunch, crunch of my own footsteps.

When I came upon the lake, I stopped and stared. Gosh, it was beautiful! A small aqua blue lake in a grassy meadow surrounded on three sides by a snow capped ridge. And a stream flowing from the snowy ridge, across the meadow and into the lake.

Hypnotized by the beauty before me, I forgot about my earlier plan to fish for trout. I walked to the grassy meadow and gazed into the stream. The water in the stream was so crystal clear that the sand particles below the water sparkled in the sunlight. Then I noticed that the stream meandered back and forth through the meadow. First turning left, then right, then left again. Like nature's own big beautiful water slide.

"Water slide, of course!" I took off all of my clothes, ran to the top of the stream, and jumped into the icy water. Down, down, down, I rode in the icy water. Bending left, then right, then left, then right again. Stark naked and shivering, I rode the stream three times. Or maybe four. I warmed up by laying out in the sun for a while. Then I ate my sandwich.

About the time I finished my sandwich, I remembered that I had hiked up to the lake to fish. So I put on my clothes and walked over to the lake. I fished for an hour or so, caught three trout and I felt moderately successful. Then I hiked back down to the campground where I cooked and ate my catch. I spent that evening staring into the campfire, reflecting on the wonderful time I'd had up at the lake.

I think about that day often. Perhaps it was the most beautiful day I'd ever spent in the mountains. And I can't explain it, but I think that my being alone up there made it better than it would have been if I'd been with another person. Because, in a way, I wasn't really alone. I was with the stream, and the lake, and the snow-capped ridge. And I had experienced an intense feeling of freedom. Freedom to take off all of my clothes and plunk myself down in the ice cold water. And to ride down the stream and to shiver from the cold. And to lay, stark naked and lizard-like, out in the sunshine. And to do so just because I felt like it. And I didn't have to explain any of it to anyone.

The Three Ages of Man

In the spring of 1994, I flew up to San Jose Airport to work with a client in Palo Alto. The fellow seated next to me on the airplane watched intently as I worked on my laptop computer. Finally, he said, "My friends tell me I ought to get one of those computers and learn how to use it."

I replied with the obvious question, "Why don't you?"

He answered, "Because it's too late. I'm over fifty now, and I'm not about to learn anything new."

I immediately snapped back, "Hey, I'm over fifty. Here's my computer!"

He and I had little to say to each other during the remainder of the flight. I continued working on my computer; he studied the in-flight magazine.

Upon landing in San Jose, I picked up a rental car, drove to Palo Alto, checked into my hotel, and decided I had just enough time to go for a run before sunset. As my hotel was only about a mile and a half from Stanford University, I was soon running on the campus.

As I ran, I thought about the fellow on the airplane. And how he figured that being fifty represented, for him, a time to quit. I got to thinking about age. Specifically about the three ages of man. It seems to me that each of us has, not one age, but three. The way I see it, we each have a chronological age, a physiological age, and a psychological age.

Our chronological age is the one we're reminded of continually. It's there on our driver's license. Demographers use it to put us into categories. We celebrate it as our birthday. It ticks by a year at a time. It's the age that the fellow on the airplane and I spoke of when we noted that we were both over fifty.

Our physiological age relates to our physical condition. It's the age so many of us struggle to keep as low as possible. We pay attention to diet; we exercise at the health club; we run around the Stanford University campus.

Our psychological age is a reflection of our disposition and attitude toward life. It's the age that we think, feel, and behave. As such, it's very much a state of mind. Recall the saying, "You're as old as you feel"? Well, that saying is, to a large extent, psychological.

We have no control over our chronological age. My chronological clock started ticking at 7:00 PM EST on December 12, 1941. It ticks away a year at a time every single year, and there isn't a thing in the world I can do about it.

We have some control over our physiological age. We can stay "physically young" through diet and exercise. We all know people who are in great shape at sixty or seventy. And we've probably known people who were in terrible shape at thirty. Clearly, we're not in complete control over our physiological age. Some of us are born healthier, more perpetually young than others. Some of it is simply "the luck of the draw."

We're in almost complete control of our psychological age. Again, "we're as old as we feel." If we think of ourselves as young and active, then that's what we are psychologically. The fellow on the airplane thought of himself as old in his fifties; I thought of myself as young in my fifties.

Quite a few years ago—I was about thirty-five chronological years old at the time—I, along with fourteen others climbed North Palisades Mountain in the California Sierras. One of the climbers, obviously older (chronologically) than the rest of us, seemed extremely strong. In spite of his age, he was quite capable of keeping up with the rest of us on even the most difficult sections of the climb. More than once, he stopped to help a fellow climber who was in just a bit "over her head."

When we arrived at the summit early that afternoon, the packs dropped and the cameras appeared for the inevitable summit shots. Then we all settled down for a well-deserved lunch of sandwiches, fruit, and water. Except for the older gentleman. He reached into his pack, pulled out a bottle of wine and fifteen small plastic glasses. Then he asked us to help him celebrate his sixty-third birthday.

I clearly remember sitting on that 14,248-foot peak, sipping my tiny share of birthday wine, staring with admiration at that older gentleman. And thinking, *Mister, when I'm sixty-three years old, I want to be just like you.* ➤

Chapter 19

Keeping Score

I **HAD DECIDED TO DRIVE** out to the desert for some target practice. So I packed my .22 rifle and ammunition and tossed a sack of empty soda pop cans into the car.

I drove off on a fairly decent dirt road fifteen miles or so east of Twentynine Palms, California. I set up the cans about eighty or one hundred feet away, loaded my rifle, and began shooting at the Pepsi can farthest to the right. I squeezed off the first round. Bang! But the can didn't move at all. I thought, *Oh well, that was just the first shot. I'll try again.*

Bang! Again, the can didn't move. Then a third shot. Still, the can didn't move. After my fourth shot, I simply couldn't believe I was that much "off." So with my rifle under my arm, I walked up to the can to investigate. And I found, to my delight, exactly four neat round holes in the Pepsi can. I'd hit the can with all four shots.

The reason the can didn't jump, I discovered, was because it was constructed of aluminum so thin that the bullet easily pierced the can without moving it at all.

Among the six or eight cans I brought along as targets was one that had earlier contained V-8 Juice. And that can, though also made of aluminum, was of heavier material. So I figured I'd try shooting at it. I stepped back the eighty or one hundred feet, took aim, and squeezed off a shot. Sure enough, the can fell over and rolled back about two feet. Another shot and the can hopped into the air about a foot or so. Then another … whoops, I missed. Then another … got it that time. I spent quite some time shooting at this one can. Until, finally, it was so badly deformed that I had to shoot at some of the others.

Driving back from the desert, I thought about the pleasure of "going for the action." About having some inanimate aluminum cylinder jump into the air and announce, "Atta boy, Bill, you got me again." It occurred to me that making the can jump was a whole lot more fun than keeping score by shooting at a paper target with a bunch of numbers on concentric rings. Without any interest in keeping score, I had had a marvelous time.

Another 4.7 Miles South

One Saturday morning, I went out for a bike ride on southern California's Pacific Coast Highway. It was a gloriously beautiful morning with just a bit of a fall chill in the air. With no particular destination in mind, I peddled south through Newport Beach. As I approached the intersection at Jamboree Road, the light turned red, so I applied my brakes and came to a stop beside the curb.

Within just a few seconds, another cyclist came to a stop beside me. I turned to him and said, "Good morning. Great day, isn't it?"

He said, "Yeah, it's nice."

I asked him, "Where did you start riding from this morning?"

He replied, "Seal Beach."

So I asked, "Where are you headed?"

He looked down at the cyclometer mounted on his handlebar and said, "Another 4.7 miles south, then I'll turn around and go back."

I smiled and nodded, acknowledging that I heard what he said. But I didn't reply. The light turned green and he sped away.

I was really surprised by the fellow's answer, "Another 4.7 miles south, then turn around." This guy was so very focused on peddling a specific distance, that I wondered if he were actually enjoying his ride.

It seems to me that we creatures of modern society possess a burning desire to quantify things. As if it doesn't count if we can't put a number on it. Like the bicyclist setting out to peddle a specific distance. Not just going for a ride for the fun of it, but needing to accomplish some quantified objective.

Now don't get me wrong. I'm not saying there's anything wrong with committing to accomplish a quantified objective. That's fine. Except that, all too often, we vastly overdo it. We tend to think of a person as successful if they've accomplished some specific number. Then they get "up on the scoreboard."

Perhaps we're so driven by numbers because numbers are easy to communicate. Like, "How was your bike ride?"

"Great, I rode twenty-seven miles."

The problem with such focus on numbers is that we lose track of an activity's essence. That is, we forget that bike riding is supposed to be enjoyable. Seems to me that we ought to be happy while we peddle our way through a beautiful morning.

But we can't quantify happiness. Thus, we can't easily communicate happiness. "How happy were you on your bike ride this morning?"

"Oh pretty happy." Or, "Very happy." Or, "Happier than when I rode last Monday."

See? It's a lot tougher to quantify happiness than it is success. And therefore, we tend to focus on success. In fact, far too often, far too many of us seek success rather than happiness. And that's a bad deal. Because in our hurried attempts to achieve success, we can so easily compromise our happiness. We become all too busy in an attempt to accomplish something, and to accumulate the trappings of success, that we don't save time for, or even stop to think about, happiness. Maybe if we were a little less busy, perhaps then we'd be happier.

Too Damn Busy

Following my daylong meeting, I returned to my guest room in the San Francisco Marriott Hotel. As I approached the door to my room, I reached into my jacket pocket and took out my room key. As the Marriott was a modern hotel, the key was an electronic card. I inserted the card into the slot on the door. Oh oh, a red light rather than green. I tried twice more. Each time, a red light. The door didn't open.

Hmmm … I figured I'd have to go back down to the reception desk to have my key reprogrammed. So I started down the hallway toward the elevator. But I stopped suddenly, for a new thought had popped into my head. I wondered, *What if I reached into the other pocket of my jacket and found another key from the Marriott Hotel? What if that second key then opened my door? Perhaps the key I earlier tried had been from a previous trip to the same hotel.*

Well guess what? Yep, you're right. I found a second Marriott key in my other pocket. And yes, it opened the door.

Man, I thought, *I'm traveling too much. I'm way too busy.*

I continued to think of myself as "too busy" until a week later when I bumped into Jerry at the airport. Jerry was *really* too busy.

Jerry and I first met as neighbors in the late 1960s. And for the next twenty-five or thirty years, we'd run into each other every once in a while. When we saw each other at the airport, he and I were waiting to board the same flight.

"Hey Jerry, how are you doing?" I asked.

"Hi, Bill. I'm fine. Long time no see," he replied.

"Looks like you and I are on the same flight to Dallas," I said. "Is that your final destination?"

Jerry thought as he replied, "No, I'm going on to … ugh … ugh …" After a ten-second pause, he remembered, "I'm going on to Memphis."

Seemed strange that Jerry was about to board a plane and couldn't more easily recall his final destination. But there was good reason for that. Jerry was awfully busy. He had a background in engineering, and had become quite the expert in computer software. His specialty was spreadsheet software. Way back in the early 1980s, Dun and Bradstreet (D&B) contracted with Jerry to teach their seminars on the use of the Lotus 1-2-3 software package. Later, when Microsoft Excel became the spreadsheet of choice, Jerry taught D&B seminars on the use of that product.

Jerry explained, "I generally fly out to some distant city on a Sunday and teach the two-day D&B course on Monday and Tuesday. Then on Tuesday night, I fly to another city to teach the same course on Wednesday and Thursday. I fly home on Thursday night. Last year, I did that forty-five weeks of the year.

Jerry went on to explain that he'd already logged sixty thousand frequent flyer miles that year—it was mid-April. He pulled his itinerary from his briefcase. It listed his teaching assignments for the rest of the year. His itinerary, printed on computer fanfold paper, reached to the floor.

Jerry told me, "A week ago, I was eating dinner in a hotel restaurant. I finished my meal and wrote on my bill, 'Charge to room 1806.' I walked to the elevator, stepped inside, and reached up to push the button for the eighteenth floor. But I couldn't find a button for the eighteenth floor. In fact, the hotel had only twelve floors. I suppose, a day or perhaps a week earlier, I stayed in room 1806 in some other hotel. As my room key didn't have a room number imprinted on it, I walked up to the desk, identified myself and asked the desk clerk to tell me my room number. Then I returned to the restaurant to clear up the matter of my dinner bill."

Noticing that Jerry had put on some weight, I asked, "Do you manage to get any exercise?"

"No, just walking from the airplane to ground transportation and pacing back and forth in front of the classroom." Jerry went on to explain, "It's generally quite late when I land at an airport. So, from the airport, I immediately call the hotel asking to speak with someone in the restaurant. By that hour, the restaurant is often closed, so I have to persuade them to cook dinner for me. I say that I'm on my way from the airport and will soon arrive at the hotel. I generally ask for salad, soup, steak, and lobster. After all, D&B is paying for it. Why shouldn't I treat myself?"

I asked Jerry, "Do you enjoy being so busy?"

"Oh no, I don't find it fun anymore. I'm pretty tired of the travel. On Fridays, I do some consulting for local clients. Help a few local firms with their computer system. But I'm too busy to send them an invoice. In fact, I haven't billed a client since August. One client said he doesn't want my charges accumulating. So he sends me a thousand dollar check each month. I don't send him an invoice or anything."

Aware of my temptation to impose my own value system on Jerry, I went pretty easy with my suggestion, "You know, Jerry, you may have the opportunity to cut back a bit on your teaching and expand your local consulting business."

"Yeah, I know. But teaching the seminar is so lucrative." Jerry went on to explain how D&B paid him a basic teaching fee plus an additional amount for each attendee beyond the first ninety. He said he earned about two hundred thousand dollars a year.

But who cares? What kind of a life is it when a guy lives in ... hey, I almost forgot the most important part of the story: Jerry has a wife and three kids. His kids' ages, at the time, were six, seven, and ten. As we walked to the plane, he recalled, "Bill, your kids are about the same ages as mine, aren't they?"

I told him, "Yes they are. I have two boys."

He suggested, "Hey, we're going to have to get our families together.

Maybe a barbecue or something." And then he chuckled as he added, "But of course, I'm never home."

Money

I was about ten years old when I bought a gag item called a "joy buzzer." One of those wind-up springs you put in the palm of your hand, then ask a friend to "shake hands." "Buzz" goes the joy buzzer as it vibrates obnoxiously. And your friend leaps with surprise. A real fun piece of junk for a ten-year-old. Price: fifty cents. When my dad found out I'd spent half a buck on the joy buzzer, he was furious. "I'm struggling to put food on the table, and you're out wasting money on nonsense."

His response was disappointing to a ten-year-old, but Dad was right. We were poor.

My dad eked out a living in a small grocery store and our options were few. He spent his life working far too hard, for too many hours, for too little money. Vacations were short and infrequent. And low cost.

If our family had had more money, we certainly would have had more options. Those with discretionary funds can be more selective in their choice of job or business. Also, they can more freely decide where they might live. And where, when, and in what manner they vacation.

But let's keep things in perspective. Accumulating money isn't most important. Health is more important. So is freedom. Love too. And discretionary time.

Speaking of discretionary time, here's an interesting truism: As I look back on my lifetime, I recall periods during which I had some extra time, and periods during which I had some extra money. Not very often, or for very long, did I have both together. Seems a nifty trick to keep the two, discretionary time and discretionary dollars, in balance.

And here's something interesting. Once a person has "enough" money, an amount representing some level of security I suppose, each additional

149

dollar has less value than each previous dollar. That is, the next dollar brings a lesser amount of additional happiness. Sort of a diminishing value of money.

I think about this diminishing value of money whenever a bellman or a waiter offers me particularly attentive service and I reward him with a generous tip. The marginal value of that tip is greater to the waiter than it is to me—assuming, of course, that I have more money than the waiter. And since the tip's marginal value is greater for the waiter than for me, the value of the money actually increases when I give it to him. In Cusco, Peru, a few years ago, I paid 72 Peruvian soles (about $22 US) for a backpack without even bargaining with the lady in the shop. I figured, "So what if I overpaid? The extra 3 or 4 Peruvian soles are worth more to the gal in the store than to me."

And now I'll tell you something that you'd better keep a secret. Because it's heresy for a management consultant even to think what I'm about to suggest—people take money too seriously. Especially business people. In a sense, business is just a game for adults. And money is a convenient way to keep score.

Sounds stupid you say? But it isn't. Here's an example. Let's say I'm working with a client in the development of a five-year strategic plan. And the entire management team favors an objective to increase net profit by a compounded annual 10 percent.

Well, who gets the additional profit each year? Why the owner of the company, of course. Oh yes, the owner and president and son of the founder. But he's already got a big house overlooking the coast. And a cabin in the mountains. And a condo on Maui. And two late-model, luxury automobiles. Is 10 percent compound annual growth really that important to him? Seems that it is.

Will it bring his family 10 percent more happiness each year? Now that's the question that never gets asked. The 10 percent goes up on the scoreboard and no one ever asks, "Why is that important?" But remember, keep this a secret. We management consultants aren't supposed to have such thoughts.

Money brings with it a responsibility, or at least it should. That is, a challenge to use money beneficially rather than wastefully. I recall reading about the roaring twenties, that historically irresponsible decade when (a minority of very fortunate) people came into too much money too fast. One particular story told of parties where men lit their cigars with hundred dollar bills. Maybe I'm nuts, but to me, that's obscene.

You know what though? In a less obvious way, we all "burn" some money. Did I really have to buy that new television set? Wouldn't the old one have done for another year? How about the time I paid an additional sixty dollars a night so we'd have a room overlooking the ocean? And did I really need that fine bottle of wine? Were any of those expenditures absolutely necessary? No, of course not. Each was a discretionary expenditure. And if you add all of them up, I've "burned" my share of hundred dollar bills.

But maybe that's OK. Because the new television, the room overlooking the ocean, and the fine wine all brought happiness to my family and to me. And isn't that, after all, what discretionary spending is all about? "Balance," that's the word. Just so I keep it in balance. I figure that if I'm just at the point where I'm concerned about being wasteful, then I've got it in balance. ➤

Chapter 20

Dignity

MOUNT RITTER, LOCATED JUST ABOVE MAMMOTH LAKES in California's Sierra Nevada Range, rises to an elevation of 13,149 feet. In August of 1976, my friend Virgil Talbott led a Sierra Club trip to climb this majestic peak. I served as assistant leader for the climb. We had a full party of fifteen, the maximum allowed on a wilderness permit.

With the wildflowers at their peak during late summer, the hike to the base of the mountain was spectacular. We stopped by Shadow Lake long enough to enjoy a snack and catch a photo of that lake's tranquil setting. Then up to Lake Ediza where we'd camp and prepare for the next day's climb.

We made camp in a beautiful alpine setting just above the lake. There we were treated to a magnificent high altitude sunset. I took a quick dip in the ice-cold stream and then shivered as I crawled into my sleeping bag. Each of the others also went to sleep early, for the next day would be long and tiring. We'd start at 5:00 AM.

The climb up Mount Ritter was both long and technical. Leaving Lake Ediza at an elevation of 9,300 feet, we'd hike about two miles to the glacier. Then up the glacier using both ice axe and crampons. Then into a steep rock-strewn chute to the saddle between Mounts Ritter and Banner. From the saddle, we'd traverse around the mountain where we'd climb into the second available chute. Then up two rock slopes to arrive at the summit. We would use our climbing rope to set up belays on two of the pitches. All in all, a long, tough day.

As planned, we left camp about 5:00 AM, just as the sky was beginning to show first light. An hour or so later, we arrived at the glacier. Good thing we started as early as we did, for the sunlight reflecting on the snow made us uncomfortably warm, even this early in the morning. Had we been on the glacier during mid-morning, we would have been terribly hot.

At the top of the glacier, we were to enter a chute, which in most years is filled with snow. But the previous winter having provided little snow, the chute was filled with loose boulders. Thus rock fall was a significant threat.

As assistant leader, it was my job to "sweep." That is, I'd remain the last person during all of the day and make sure that the party didn't get too far "strung out." And I'd offer assistance to those having any sort of a problem, either with equipment or with the pace of the climb.

One of the climbers, a lady named Dorothy, was slow from the very start. She seemed a bit over her head both in terms of technical climbing ability and physical conditioning. She moved slowly up the glacier and needed help in taking off her crampons when we arrived at the chute.

Seated at the top of the glacier, with the loose rock chute above, Dorothy and I stopped to remove our crampons. We sat facing downhill, she immediately to my right, and both her ice axe and mine about an arm's length to my left. As the other climbers started up the chute above us, I asked them to be careful not to dislodge any loose rocks. For seated, as we were, at the bottom of the chute, Dorothy and I were most vulnerable to rock fall. I decided we'd best hurry and I said so to Dorothy. If rocks did come tumbling our way, we'd be better off standing looking up into the chute than seated looking away.

Still seated, we had removed Dorothy's crampons and were securing them to her pack when someone screamed "Rock!" About a half second later, I heard the crash, crash, crash of a boulder careening down the chute. I grabbed Dorothy around the shoulders, pulled her into my lap, and curled by upper body over hers. About then I heard a loud crash immediately to my left.

I looked left and saw that the careening boulder had crashed into her ice axe and broken the metal head off from the wooden shaft. Looking down onto the glacier, I saw the boulder skidding along the ice. It looked to be perhaps a foot or so in diameter. I shivered while thinking of how close I'd come to being hit in the back, and no doubt killed, by the boulder.

We were all glad to get to the top of the rock-strewn chute and into the saddle between the two mountains. Dorothy and I were especially glad to be looking down, rather than up, at the chute.

I helped Dorothy numerous times throughout the day. From putting on and removing crampons, to advice on foot placement on the rock pitches, to encouragement when she felt exhausted. Fortunately, Dorothy wasn't afraid of heights. So when we stopped on a wide ledge for lunch, and looked down some two thousand feet, she was fine.

It was mid-afternoon when we arrived on the summit. A glorious view and a wonderful feeling. Eating lunch on the top of Mount Ritter, we basked in both sunshine and celebration.

From the summit, we would descend by a less technical route. So technical climbing, which is always more dangerous going down, wouldn't be an issue. The challenge would be endurance. During our four-hour descent, we scrambled over and around boulders, and skirted a small glacier. Rough going yes, but more of an arduous scramble than a climb.

The roughness of the terrain, coupled with our rapidly diminishing energy, made us vulnerable to an accident. Knowing he needed to be ever so cautious, Virgil set a fairly slow pace. But the long, physically difficult day made for fifteen tired climbers. We were all looking forward to arrival in camp.

Dorothy was near exhaustion, so I did everything I could to support her. When I offered to carry her pack, she gladly accepted. We strapped her pack to mine.

It was growing dark as we approached camp. We were walking on an easy, level trail in an alpine meadow, beside the stream, which carried glacial melt down to the lake. Those up front with Virgil were already arriving in camp. Dorothy and I would be there in ten minutes or so. Oh, for a warm sleeping bag!

I stopped to admire the meandering stream and to get a cool drink. Dorothy came up to me and said, "I can take my pack now."

Wanting to be helpful, I told her, "It's OK Dorothy. I'll carry your pack to camp for you."

Hearing what I had just said, she looked disappointed. She didn't say anything, but simply turned and continued her slow walk toward camp.

And then I figured it out: Dorothy needed her dignity. She needed to walk into camp carrying her own pack. I had been so concerned about her physical need that I hadn't recognized her emotional need. Realizing my error, I hurried up to her side and said, "Here Dorothy, take your pack."

The broadest smile suddenly appeared across her tired face. Clearly she was exhausted. And she'd no doubt be stiff as heck in the morning. But for now, all was perfect for her. Following Dorothy into our now-dark camp, I was the last of our party to arrive. The end of a long, tough, and truly magnificent day.

Few others took the time to eat a real dinner. Most had a quick, cold snack and crawled into their sleeping bags. By 8:45 or so, Virgil and I sat alone, drinking tea at the campfire. We chuckled a bit about the others having gone right to sleep. Both of us felt good about the wonderful day we'd just enjoyed and about our success in leading the climb. We reflected on the various sections of the route where we were vulnerable to injury. Both of us were ever so glad to have all of our tired participants safely back at camp.

As I sipped my tea and stared into the fire, I felt good about my having helped Dorothy. And I felt especially good about her having taught me a valuable lesson. Each of us needs our dignity.

The Janitor in the Sacramento Airport

When traveling by airplane, I prefer to wear comfortable casual clothes. Generally loose fitting, cotton slacks, or shorts, in season, and tennis shoes. I learned long ago that the airline is just as happy to give me the exact same service and charge me the exact same fare whether I'm dressed comfortably or not.

When returning from a business meeting, I generally arrive at the airport dressed in business attire including jacket, tie, and leather shoes. Hardly the comfy clothes I'd prefer to wear on the flight home. The solution is simple. I arrive at the airport early enough to visit the men's room where I change clothes. For three decades or more, this has been my ritual.

Late one afternoon about 1990, I arrived at the Sacramento Airport. I was traveling home from a meeting with a client in that city and I had just enough time to change clothes before my flight. I went into the stall in the men's room toting a small carry-on suitcase in hand.

I opened the suitcase onto the floor. Then I took off my tie. Before changing slacks, I had to take off my belt and remove everything from my pockets. I reached into my right pocket and there found quite a bit of change, likely about four dollars worth. I looked for some place to put the change and noticed the stainless steel toilet paper holder. So I placed my change on top of the holder. I had planned, of course, to put the change into the pocket of the casual slacks I'd soon be wearing.

About the time I finished changing clothes, I heard someone enter the men's room. Stepping out from the stall with suitcase in hand, I saw that the person who entered was the janitor. He had just emptied the waste-basket and was starting to clean up around the sink. We said hello to each other. I mentioned my changing clothes and told him of my preference for flying in comfort. I suppose I also mentioned that I'd be flying to Orange County Airport. And that I was hoping to arrive home in time to kiss the boys goodnight before they went to sleep.

I left the men's room—you guessed it—having forgotten all about my change on top of the toilet paper holder. I had other things on my mind, like checking in for my flight and getting through the awful security line (which, looking back to the 1990s, now seems not so very awful).

I walked quite some distance across one concourse to the other. Next, I stood on line at the America West Airlines check-in counter. Then, all of a sudden, someone to my side approached me holding both of his hands out in front of him. It was the janitor from the men's room. And in his hands, he held the four dollars of change that I had mistakenly left on the toilet paper holder.

To say the least, I was surprised! Surprised for two reasons. First, this fellow was so very honest that he came looking for me to return my money. It would have been ever so easy for him to pocket the change and be four dollars richer for having done so. Second, I was surprised that this fellow walked so far to return the money. He had to hike, as I did, across one concourse to the other. But he did it.

I thanked him and offered to split the money with him. "Let's share it," I proposed. But he insisted on giving me all of my money. We argued about it for a time and, finally, I prevailed and we shared the money. No we didn't count; we simply divvied up the money by volume, about half a handful for each of us. We thanked each other and he departed. I checked into my flight, went through security, and boarded my airplane. I probably smiled during the entire hour-long flight, for I was delighted by the janitor's act of honesty. How fortunate I was to have played a role, albeit a passive one, in this small but wonderful human act.

I've told this story many times to many people over many years. And all these years I've thought of myself as a passive participant. After all, the janitor did it all by himself. I just happened to be in the right place at the right time.

And then, early one Sunday morning about ten years later, I woke up with a revelation. Maybe the janitor didn't act by himself. Maybe I acted too. Maybe it wasn't he alone who was responsible for his act of honesty. Maybe I helped precipitate the act. How? By speaking with him.

Some ten years after the janitor's act of honesty, it occurred to me that maybe very few people speak with the janitor. Perhaps my speaking with him, my sharing my preference to fly in comfort, my mentioning my looking forward to getting home to kiss my boys goodnight, maybe this brief conversation told him that I cared about him. That I valued him enough to share with him.

Perhaps the janitor walked across Sacramento Airport to return my four dollars because I had allowed him his dignity. ➤

Chapter 21

Some Things Are Important — and Some Aren't

AS A **TWENTY-TWO-YEAR-OLD ELECTRONICS ENGINEER** straight out of college, I landed a job with Beckman Instruments Company in Fullerton, California. This job would prove to be my introduction to "the real world."

Oh sure, I had a fresh diploma from engineering school. And I knew quite a bit about advanced calculus. But I had little notion of how any of my schooling applied away from the college campus—out in "the real world." And so, eager to learn, I asked questions. With questions about electrical engineering, I went to Tony, my boss and the head of the electrical engineering department. For questions about mechanics, I went to Don, the head of the mechanical engineering department, and for questions about technical drawings, I went to the jobshoppers.

Oh yeah, I need to tell you about the jobshoppers. I arrived at Beckman in 1964, in the midst of those heady days of space exploration and defense contracting. At the time, we Americans were all wrapped up in the mission of NASA, per President Kennedy's challenge of landing a man on the moon and returning him safely back to earth.

Because space and defense projects were often short term, engineering companies were reluctant to hire technical people for such work. Who knew if they'd still need that draftsman, technician, or engineer a year or two later? So engineering companies would lease, instead of hire, those persons. "Job shop agencies" would hire technical people and, in turn, lease them to engineering companies for short-to medium-term project work. A jobshopper might spend a few months at one company, then a few months at another. In the mid-1960s, jobshoppers stayed busy with space and defense work and did quite well financially.

I got along with all of the people I worked with, including the jobshoppers. In fact, I got along with them famously. Ed Jaglie was a jolly fat fellow from Germany who had the most infectious laugh and a terrific sense of humor. I could count on him for a great story perhaps two or three times each week. And Bill Pearson loved to hike. So he and I did three or four weekend trips out to the San Jacinto Wilderness.

A new jobshopper named Sherm came to work with us about the time a friend of mine had a serious auto accident in Albuquerque. Sherm got word of my planning a weekend trip to visit my friend in Albuquerque's Regional Hospital. Having known me for only one week, Sherm offered, "I have about five hundred dollars in savings. If you'd like to borrow some money to make your trip, I'd be happy to lend it to you." I was so very touched by his offer but I declined. I too had some money, though not nearly five hundred dollars, in savings.

After working at Beckman for a few months, I noticed that some of the managers acted sort of snooty. For example, a few of the upper level managers would wear their suit coat to walk down the hall to the bathroom. And, trying to act more upper level I suppose, some of the mid-level managers did the same.

I also noticed another kind of snooty behavior. I heard one of the managers speak critically of a senior technician. The criticism was that the technician was doing engineering work but didn't have an engineering degree. Seemed silly to me because the technician was a very bright fellow and had actually been doing an outstanding job.

Though I noticed these pretentious acts, I tried to ignore them. Certainly they didn't affect me. I did my work, I asked questions of anyone who might have the information I needed, and I enjoyed friendly relationships with all of my co-workers.

One day, Bill Pearson, the jobshopper with whom I hiked, sat with me in the company cafeteria. Clear out of the blue, he asked me, "Do you know why the jobshoppers like you so much?"

I was shocked by his question. Sure, I knew that I got along with these guys real well. We laughed, and we joked. They were all nice guys and I suppose I was a nice guy too. But what did Bill mean by "… they like me so much"? His question made me feel somehow special and, at the same time, embarrassed.

Bill explained, "Here at Beckman, there's sort of a caste system. Most of the managers and engineers think they're higher and mightier than the others. They consider those without a degree, especially an engineering degree, to be lower. And we jobshoppers, those of us who aren't actually employees of the company, they consider lowest of all."

Bill added, "If an engineer has a question for which a jobshopper might have the answer, the engineer wouldn't ask the jobshopper. He might search for the answer among his fellow degreed engineers or simply go without an answer."

"You're different though," said Bill. "You don't care about any of that caste system crap. If you want to know something, you'll ask whomever you figure might have the answer. And you pay no regard to rank or caste or any other aspect of company politics. And that's why the jobshoppers like you so much."

Both surprised and embarrassed by what Bill had just told me, I simply smiled and said, "Thank you." I didn't realize at the time, for I was young and naïve, but I allowed the jobshoppers their dignity. And I did it so easily. I simply ignored a whole bunch of crap that wasn't important at all.

The Young Hotshot on Mopah Peak

Located in California's eastern Mojave Desert, Mopah Peak rises to an elevation of 3,530 feet. Certainly it isn't very high, but it's a fun scramble and, if climbing it for the first time, quite a challenge in route finding. It's actually a volcanic plug that looks just like a candle. Not a new candle of perfectly cylindrical shape, but a candle that's been burned once or twice. Burned so that a steep river of wax has melted a groove down one side of the candle. And a pile of wax "rubble" has accumulated at the base.

If you substitute a steep rock chute for the river of wax down the side, and you replace the wax rubble with rock rubble, that's Mopah Peak. Upon seeing the peak for the first time, I gasped, "On my gosh, it's straight up. How in the world can we climb that?" But it's really quite doable. You simply have to walk around the peak until you find the steep chute. Then work your way up the chute and figure out which rock wall near the top of the chute is climbable.

I climbed Mopah Peak for the first time with Mark Hurst in December of 1976. Immediately it became one of my favorites and I returned to climb it perhaps another half dozen times. On one occasion, I led the climb as an official Sierra Club trip with fourteen or fifteen participants. Among the participants was a young fellow named Michael. He was in good physical condition and quite a capable climber. Honestly though, I found him irritating because he was one of those young hotshots who thought he knew everything. And he spoke almost constantly. And almost always boastfully.

Typical of capable young hotshots, he had to stay right up there with the leader. So throughout our hike to the peak, he was at my side or on my heals, boasting of his accomplishments. Were I a participant rather than a leader, I could have escaped. I would have dropped back in our line of hikers to avoid him. But as the leader, I was stuck with this fellow for the day because I was obliged to walk up front, and there was certainly no way that Michael would ever drop back in line.

As we approached the peak to begin our climb, I overheard him telling another participant that, on any climb, it's important for the leader to be the first to step on the summit. I wondered, *What the hell is that about?* Seemed silly to me, but not wanting to encourage conversation with him, I ignored his remark.

We came upon a clearing and got our first look at the peak. Some of the party remained speechless while a few others exclaimed, "Oh my gosh!" I assured them that the climb wasn't nearly as impossible as it appeared.

All went well. We had a good, capable group and we worked our way up the chute in good time. Two hours later, we stood just below a thirty-foot wall where we'd need a belay—protection of the climbing rope.

I climbed to the top of the wall and set up the belay. I anchored myself to a large boulder, sat down, and passed one end of the rope around my lower back. I then tossed the other end of the rope down for the next climber to tie in.

As I expected, the first to tie in was our young hotshot. "On belay?" he shouted.

I replied, "Belay is on."

Just as I expected, he climbed up quite fast. Once on top and at my side, he requested, "Off belay?"

"Belay is off," I replied.

He untied from the rope and, as soon as he did, I pointed toward a broad, flat area and instructed him to, "Go sit over there."

I tossed the rope back down and we repeated this belaying process one climber at a time.

Climbing rocks is inherently a slow process. The leader has to set up the belay, then a climber has to tie in, make his or her way up the rock face, then untie. The leader then has to repeat this same belay-climbing process for each and every climber. For a party of fifteen or so, we'd be working this wall for well over an hour. So after about half of our party had climbed up and were sitting with Michael in the flat area, I figured I'd relieve their boredom. I'd simply send them up the safe and easy friction climb to the summit.

It occurred to me that I had the perfect opportunity to teach Michael a lesson about what was and wasn't important. So I turned to him and asked, "Say, Michael, would you lead the first half of our party to the summit?"

A look of both surprise and delight appeared immediately across his face. He hopped to his feet encouraging the others to do likewise. And away they scampered.

About forty minutes later, the rest of us arrived at the summit. I stepped up to Michael and said, "Thank you for leading the group to the summit. I appreciate your help."

As we shook hands, he said, "I'm happy to help."

But I wonder if he understood the lesson I hoped to teach. I wonder if he realized that being the first in the party to step on the summit isn't among the most important things in the world. I guess Michael is now in his mid-fifties. I'm sure he remembers our day together on Mopah Peak. But I wonder *how* he remembers it. Certainly he remembers it as a fun climb. But does he remember it simply as one more accomplishment about which he can boast? Or has he grown too old to boast? I wonder if he thinks back on that day and reflects on an important lesson he then learned. I hope so. ➤

Chapter 22

Death

S OME YEARS AGO, A FRIEND OBSERVED that whenever we experience a major tragedy, we forever remember where we were and what we were doing at the time.

He's right.

I was in New York in November of 1963 when President Kennedy was killed. I recall huddling amongst fifty or sixty other college students, by a convertible automobile, listening to the radio news broadcast.

In April of 1968, I was in Washington, D.C. during that city's riot following Martin Luther King's death. I was traveling by train, from Richmond, Virginia, to Washington, D.C. when King was killed. I stepped out of the train station into a full-scale riot in the streets of our nation's capital. A sad and frightening experience.

On September 11, 2001, I woke up at 5:30 AM. The hotel's health club opened at 6:00 AM, so I spent a half hour preparing for the second day of the three-day course I was teaching in San Francisco.

I arrived at the health club at 6:05 AM. The television was on. I stared in disbelief watching an enormous fire engulf the upper floors of one of the towers of New York's World Trade Center. Before I could even wonder what might have caused such an enormous fire, the newscaster said, "We don't mean to alarm you, but another airplane is approaching the towers." I then watched that airplane crash into the second tower.

I stared at the television screen for an hour. I believed what I saw, and yet, I disbelieved what I saw.

Back in my room after a shower, I checked for phone messages. My wife, Wendy, had called earlier. Her voice sounded terrible. Of course it did. I called her back. She was crying. She asked, "What's happening? What's becoming of us?" I wish I could have found an answer to make her feel better. I couldn't. She was worried about our friends in New York. She'd try to call them. We'd speak again later.

I really wanted to be home with Wendy.

I walked from my hotel near Union Square to my classroom at the Marriott Hotel, about a half-mile. The streets of San Francisco seemed less busy than usual. Maybe. I wasn't sure. Quieter anyway.

While teaching the class, my mind was elsewhere. In lower Manhattan. Same with all of the course attendees. It was hard to work. Hard to concentrate. I occurred to me that nothing I was doing was important. And how many people were trapped in the stairwells of those two giant buildings? And what was it like on those airplanes—just before the end?

I spent that evening walking the streets of San Francisco. I had done so a hundred times before. But that evening was different. I didn't enjoy the walk. I didn't want to be in San Francisco. I wanted to be home with Wendy.

The financial district was like a ghost town. The high-rise office buildings had been closed that day. The banks, the Pacific Stock Exchange. Very few people in the streets. Many of the shops were closed. Handwritten signs read, "Closed, out of respect." A large American flag flew at half-mast, just above street level, in front of a high-rise building. I looked up at the building. I remember thinking that, in New York, this building would be considered "smaller."

I walked to Chinatown. There, in a Chinese language newspaper taped to a store window, were photographs of the burning towers. Those who could read the language huddled around—very much like we college students, years earlier, had huddled around a car radio to learn the details of President Kennedy's assassination.

Dinner was not memorable.

I walked back to the hotel. I called my son Larry. He was at home near his college campus. We spoke of the tragedy in New York. He'd been watching television after class and was alarmed to learn that, in at least one part of the world, people danced in the streets in celebration of the tragedy in America. I assured him that we Americans were different. No matter how angry we might become, we would never celebrate another's pain, as those others did. I thought what I told him was true. I wanted it to be true. What kind of a world had I brought my sons into? What were the answers to Wendy's questions, "What's happening to us? What's becoming of us?"

I called my son Doug in his college dormitory. One of the boys who lived in Doug's dorm had lost his father that morning. Seems that the young man's dad was on the airplane that crashed into the second tower in New York. I had watched that happen while at the health club that morning. I had watched this young man's father die. *Hell, I wish I were home with Wendy. What in the world am I doing in San Francisco anyway? Nothing I'm doing is important.*

I kept waking up that night wondering how many people were trapped in the stairwells of those two giant buildings. And what was it like on those airplanes—just before the end?

Yea, Trevor

I don't know how many soldiers were riding on that truck that morning, but when the roadside bomb exploded, only Trevor was killed. I think it happened just outside of Tikrit, but I'm really not sure. Yes, I read the articles in the newspaper, but each time I saw Trevor's name, my eyes filled with tears. So I missed a lot of the details.

Trevor was twenty-two years old, the same age as my son Doug. In fact, Trevor and Doug were classmates in high school. But it was actually through my son Larry that I knew Trevor. Larry and Trevor were teammates on the high school's hockey team. I remember all those games on all those evenings. And all of us parents standing shoulder to shoulder rooting for our team. For our kids. "Yea, Larry." "Yea, Trevor."

Two days after Doug's college graduation, we went to Trevor's funeral at the church. It was just as you'd expect: Trevor's coffin draped in an American flag, military color guard, and a lot of people in a lot of pain.

You know, when an older person dies, folks tell about those eighty-seven Thanksgivings gone by, and all those summer campouts with the grandkids, and those times when we were all much younger, way back most of our life ago. And not that we're happy for the death, of course, but somehow or another, an older person dying kind of makes sense. Like maybe it's OK. But when a young person dies, nothing is OK. Nothing.

A few days after Trevor's funeral, I went out for a bike ride. I'm not sure why, but I peddled by Trevor's house. And then I peddled over to Huntington Beach. To the rink where the boys used to play hockey. And I thought about all those games on all those evenings. And all of us parents standing shoulder to shoulder, rooting for our team. For our kids. "Yea, Larry." "Yea, Trevor."

Yea, Trevor.

Mister Wilson

The veterinarian said the injection was quite lethal and that it would all be over in an instant. She was right. Mister Wilson stopped purring right away. He laid his head down and that was the end.

Wendy cried. I did too.

I can certainly understand Wendy's crying. She loved that old cat. And he loved her. Their mutual affection began when he was just four years old. The way I heard the story, she got Mister Wilson from a family whose large dog was interested in devouring him. The first time she picked up that docile old black and white fur ball, he put his paws around her neck and purred so the neighbors could hear him. Her heart melted and she took him home. That was sixteen years earlier. And I couldn't count the number of times the two of them repeated that same tender scene during all those years.

She and he had been through some tough times together. Mostly emergency visits to the veterinarian when Mister Wilson's chronic asthma condition acted up. She worried about him more and more as he grew older. And slower. And weaker.

He was so very devoted to her. No matter where he happened to be in the house or in the yard, when she got home from work, he'd run to the door to greet her. In the kitchen, he'd remain under foot, in the way, for most of the evening. She was there, so he was too.

But I'll be damned if I know why I cried. As a boy, I had a dog, not a cat. In fact, I never even *knew* a cat until I married Wendy and thereby got related to Mister Wilson.

Come to think of it, Mister Wilson and I spent quite a bit of time together. I could count on him to appear in the kitchen whenever I took the can opener out of the drawer. He especially liked tuna fish. I like tuna fish too, so Mister Wilson and I often ate lunch together.

But his favorite food was smoked chicken. Whenever I'd have a chicken smoking in the barbecue, he'd lie down nearby and wait. He had to be right there when the chicken was ready. He'd follow me—and the smoked chicken—into the house to collect his reward for having stood guard for three hours or so. Mister Wilson sure could eat smoked chicken!

Often he'd keep me company in my home office. He'd station himself on the floor, at times beneath my chair, approximately where I would have liked to have placed my feet. And he enjoyed sitting on my lap while I wrote articles. Hearing me typing on the keyboard, he'd amble into my office and stand there looking up at me. Naturally, I'd continue to type while trying my best to ignore him.

But my ignoring never lasted very long. He'd soon signal me with his loud, low-toned meow. I'd look down at him and into those huge, black eyes, and the ignoring was over. I'd pick him up, place him on my lap, and there he'd sit, or at times, stand, purring so the neighbors could hear him. I actually got used to typing with my elbows stuck out to the side. More than once, I told Wendy, "Mister Wilson helped me write an article today."

Actually, this is the first time I've ever written about Mister Wilson. And my elbows aren't stuck out to the side—because he's not here in my lap. You know something? I think I miss the little guy. ➤

Part Five

Adventure Retirement

BY THE TIME I REACHED my sixty-third birthday, both Larry and Doug had graduated from college and embarked on their own career paths. Wendy, my second wife, and I had been happily married for eleven years. And with the boys off on their own, our large, five-bedroom home was clearly too big for just the two of us.

Wendy had been self-employed as a family law attorney for twenty-five years, and I as a management consultant for twenty-five. We both felt the need for a change. All that we needed to trigger that change was some catalyst.

In the spring of 2005 we found that catalyst—over there in the far corner of the room.

Chapter 23

Our Need for Change

WENDY AND I HAD PROMISED OURSELVES, were we ever to retire, that ours would be an active, adventurous retirement. In fact, we avoided using the word retirement. Instead, we'd refer to "the next chapter in our lives."

I, especially, was tired of living in Southern California. Tired of the traffic, of course. And the crowds. And the high price of just about everything. And I was bothered by ostentatious people. It seemed to me that so many people in coastal Orange County, California, had fifty cents more than their next-door neighbor. And darn if they didn't have to show it off.

For some years, Wendy and I had been trying to define "the next chapter in our lives." Our discussions had generally focused on where we'd like to live. We both favored a smaller community with nearby outdoor activities. During our vacations, we explored various communities, wondering what it might be like to live there.

We both realized that moving on to our next chapter would involve more than simply selecting a pretty place with fewer people and a mountain range nearby. There was also the question, "What will we do when we get there?" Wendy, especially, wanted to do volunteer work, to help people and to benefit society. Going for five hikes a week wasn't to be the next chapter in her life.

As the entrepreneur in the family, I was trying to figure out some sort of a business we could manage while living in a smaller community. In fact, I probably came up with a new business idea about once each month.

On one particular evening in April 2005, I announced at dinner that I had come up with a super-great idea. Thanks, in part, to two glasses of wine, I was especially enthusiastic about my latest inspiration. "It was the perfect on-line business," I promised.

But in my enthusiasm, I made one serious mistake. I said, "This business is so portable, we could run it on a laptop computer, on a dining room table, in a travel trailer, in a National Park." I was absolutely beaming as I awaited Wendy's enthusiastic response.

But Wendy's response was far from enthusiastic. She said she didn't want to live a nomadic life in a travel trailer. That she wanted to be of help to people. That she didn't want to work with them from afar, over the Internet. Instead, she wanted to help them while looking them right in the eye. Hmmm … we were far from being in agreement.

Before too long, Wendy found her way over to the computer searching online for opportunities to help people. Kind of like the Peace Corps does. Still reeling from disappointment, I followed along and looked over her shoulder at the computer screen. I may even have carried a glass of wine in my hand.

Wendy actually came up with some interesting stuff. A number of opportunities to go here or there in the world, work for six to twelve weeks as a volunteer, and pay four thousand dollars or so for the privilege of doing so. An interesting vacation to be sure, but hardly a new chapter in our lives. Wendy printed out some of the more interesting web pages and started a file called Volunteer Opportunities.

That night, lying in bed, trying to fall asleep, I wondered how I had so messed up in presenting my wonderful business idea.

The United States Peace Corps

A day or so later, I found an announcement in the newspaper about a retirement fair on the campus of the University of California-Irvine. Five bucks. Heck, we could afford that. And so we signed up.

The retirement fair occupied three rooms, each dedicated separately to: Work Opportunities in Retirement; Learn and Play Opportunities in Retirement; Volunteer Opportunities in Retirement.

Because it was closest to the men's room, I found it most convenient to begin in the Volunteer Opportunities room. There were perhaps a dozen booths in the room, each manned by a person or two. Most of the booths described local volunteer opportunities in and around Orange County. Like "Help Save the Newport Back Bay." Knowing full well that the next chapter in my life wouldn't be anywhere near Newport Back Bay, I attempted to scurry along. But Wendy's sense of completeness dictated that we visit every booth. And so we did.

Finally, we approached the very last booth, way back in the corner of the room. It described volunteer opportunities in the United States Peace Corps. Wendy said to the fellow manning the booth, "I didn't know that the Peace Corps was interested in seniors becoming volunteers."

The smiling recruiter whose name tag read Allan replied, "Oh yes, the Peace Corps is very interested in seniors. Because they have so much life experience to offer."

Wendy and I spent the next twenty minutes speaking with Allan. He filled our plastic retirement fair shopping bags with brochures, booklets, and applications. We thanked him for his time, shook his hand, and walked out the door. As we left the building, I turned to Wendy and asked, "Are you interested in the Peace Corps Volunteer opportunity?"

"Yes," she replied, "are you?"

I said, "Yes."

Apparently we were both very interested because we spent that evening reading over the Peace Corps publications. Within two days, we were filling out our applications. Within a week, we called our friend Linda, a real estate agent, and asked her to list our house for sale.

While Wendy and I were both seriously interested in joining the Peace Corps, we actually had different motivations. Her motivation was more in line with the mission of the Peace Corps. She wanted to go somewhere in the world to help people in need.

My motivation was twofold: First, I was ready for a change, and a Peace Corps assignment in some third-world nation would certainly offer that. Second, I saw this as an opportunity for adventure. And I thought immediately, and narrowly, of an assignment in Latin America.

The only Latin American country with which I was familiar was Mexico. I had traveled in Mexico numerous times and found the country to be, not only enchanting, but also offering great adventure. I assumed the same would be true of other nations in Latin America. Also, the Spanish language had been a hobby of mine since I was in my twenties. So I viewed an assignment in Latin America as an opportunity to enjoy speaking Spanish and to advance my skills in the language.

While Wendy was willing to serve anywhere in the world where people needed help, she appreciated my interest in Latin America. So she agreed to check "Preference for Latin America" on her Peace Corps application.

The Peace Corps warned their applicants, "Don't assume you'll be accepted into the Peace Corps. Some people aren't. Don't quit your job or sell your house." Allan, our Peace Corps recruiter, offered us a very specific warning about the Peace Corps' medical department. He said that the medical department was a bureaucracy. And especially tough when screening seniors. Seems that while the Peace Corps recruiters were working hard to develop volunteers among the senior community, the Peace Corps' medical department was working hard to reject them. Allan warned, "For sure, don't sell your home."

In spite of this warning, both Wendy and I shut down our businesses and we sold our home.

Given the timing of the application process, we expected to leave for an assignment in the spring of 2006. So we spent December and January packing up all of our possessions to store them away for a few years. Wendy had suggested that, while we were waiting for our assignment, we should take a driving trip around the United States to say goodbye to all of our family and friends.

That sounded pretty good to me. A winter trip in the old, four-wheel drive Landcruiser. Around the whole country. With tire chains and sleeping bags in the car—just in case. Yeah, a neat adventure, let's do it!

We worked like soldiers packing boxes, arranging for the moving van, donating furniture to charities and books to the public library. We even sold Wendy's car. We'd buy her another when we returned from Latin America a few years later.

Also, we threw out a whole bunch of stuff. I'll bet that, on a tonnage basis, we dumped more stuff than we kept.

Reaction to the News

I feared that our friends would laugh at us when we told them we were joining the Peace Corps. But I was wrong. Almost all of our friends were supportive. In fact, most were excited for us.

Sue Padernacht smiled and looked me straight in the eye when she said, "You're so cool!" She made me feel … well, "cool."

Randy Roth was ever so enthusiastic. Turns out that he had served in the Peace Corps in Costa Rica when he was twenty-two years old. He told an interesting story about having introduced a Costa Rican boy to classical music. The boy, years later, went on to receive his Doctorate Degree in the History of Classical Music at the University of Southern California. Neat.

Bob Parker said he was happy for us. He told us that he too would have liked to join the Peace Corps. But he "didn't have the guts." He wasn't willing to give up his comfortable life in the United States.

My dad, then ninety-three years old, was pleased about our joining the Peace Corps. He said that what we were doing was "a nice gesture." He was proud that we were volunteering to help people.

I was actually afraid to tell Larry and Doug. Oh, maybe not afraid, but at least apprehensive. I worried about how they'd take it. I mean, our going away, not being right there to support them as we'd always been.

But they were both in their mid-twenties. They both had graduated from college and had started down their own career paths. They'd do fine with our being a continent away. And our joining the Peace Corps might provide a good model for the boys. We could show them that even "old folks" can keep adventuring. But how would they react to the news?

Their reaction was great! Yes, they were quite surprised. Larry kept repeating "this is big!" But he was truly happy for us. Figured we'd do just great as Peace Corps volunteers.

Doug's response was absolutely the most positive of all whom we told. In a voice uncharacteristically loud for Doug, he almost shouted, "That's outstanding!" He bubbled over with excitement.

Both boys agreed that Wendy and I should try for an assignment in a beach community with great surf. Then they'd visit us often. We promised that we'd do our best to land an assignment in such a location.

Just a few people weren't supportive of our decision to join the Peace Corps. Dick Brugman said, "I don't know what to say, Bill."

I figured that was a polite way of telling me he thought I was nuts. And

Ed Carver told me, "Be very, very careful. You could disappear down there and no one would find you for months."

And one friend actually did laugh at us. While laughing, Tom Jordan suggested we should instead "Drive up to Santa Ana and help Suzie figure out how to operate her restaurant. That way you don't have to leave home to help someone."

Wendy and I soon concluded that each person's reaction to our joining the Peace Corps revealed more about them than about us. Those who were adventurous were supportive. Those who were fearful stressed caution. And those who were either content or especially comfortable with their current lifestyle told us, in one way or another, that we were crazy. ➢

Chapter 24

Two Vagabonds

OUR DRIVE AROUND THE COUNTRY would include visits to family and friends in seventeen states and one Canadian province. Starting in southern California, we'd travel counter-clockwise. East to Florida, then up the Atlantic Coast to Maine. Then across the northern states to British Columbia. Then down the Pacific Coast to southern California.

And we'd do the drive in my sixteen-year-old Toyota Landcruiser. When we began our trip on January 21, 2006, the car had 206,157 miles on the odometer. We figured we'd drive about 10,000 miles. I had every confidence in the old Landcruiser. I loved (and still do love) that old car. In fact, Wendy once told me, "Someday, they'll bury you in that car."

I told her, "It's OK with me that they bury me in the Landcruiser. I just hope that it won't be during the winter of 2006."

As this would be a winter trip, we needed to prepare for weather. We packed lots of clothing plus food and water in the car. We also carried sleeping bags and a snow shovel, just in case. Plus tire chains and snow-shoes. Wouldn't we be a sight arriving at my brother Jerry's house in Lake Worth, Florida?

The Peace Corps approved Wendy's application quickly. But mine got hung up in the all-powerful bureaucracy of the Peace Corps' medical department. Seems that, when I took my medical exam, one of my three blood pressure readings was a bit high. So my doctor prescribed a blood pressure medicine.

That did it! Because I was taking blood pressure medication, the Peace Corps' medical department required that I take a whole series of tests. While visiting family in Florida, I had those tests performed during two trips to the Aventura Hospital. No matter that the various tests showed that I was fine, the Peace Corps' medical department kept asking for more and more information. They seemed impossible to satisfy. In an attempt to satisfy the Peace Corps, I incurred medical expenses totaling about twenty thousand dollars.

As this hassle with the Peace Corps' medical department dragged on, two facts were becoming clear. First, there was a very good chance that the Peace Corps would eventually deny my application. And second, even if they'd accept my application, it wouldn't be anytime soon.

And so we slowed the pace of our trip. As we were literally home-less and had absolutely no place to go, we were in no hurry to get there. What started out as a two-month winter trip stretched into seven months and spanned three seasons. As we extended the length of our trip, we also changed the nature of the trip. We drove minor, rather than major, roads and enjoyed a heavy dose of sightseeing. Our travels now featured deeper, longer visits with family and friends. When we stayed in a bed and break-fast, we'd linger in conversation with our hosts. Breakfast, at times, lasted two hours or more.

During the winter, we drove the Blue Ridge Parkway through The Smokey Mountain National Park. We visited Williamsburg, Gettysburg, and the museums and monuments in Washington, DC. Plus Ellis Island on the Hudson River and Franklin Roosevelt's home in Hyde Park, New York.

In the springtime, we visited the national and state parks of the western United States. We stayed in a cabin in South Dakota's Custer State Park. We camped at, and hiked from, Jenny Lake in The Grand Teton National Park. And we camped in a snowstorm, in our tiny backpack tent, in Yellowstone National Park.

Thinking about where we might want to settle after returning from our volunteer experience, we scoped out a number of communities. We stayed in each for two or three days checking out real estate prices, weather statistics, and opportunities for both cultural and outdoor activities.

During our long road trip, a number of people asked us, "How does it feel not having a home?" Both Wendy and I replied, "It's great!" And we meant it, as we were very much enjoying the freedom of homelessness. We could go anywhere we wanted and stay as long as we pleased. It was terrific!

On one occasion, I suggested to Wendy, "When we return to southern California, perhaps we could live under a bridge on the Santa Ana River bike trail." Wendy didn't say anything, but the look she gave me suggested that I should drop the idea.

We returned to southern California on the last day of August, some seven months and ten days after we had left. We had traveled 17,310 miles. It had been the trip of a lifetime.

Who and What I Had Missed

During our road trip, Wendy and I spoke frequently with Larry and Doug by telephone. Even so, I had missed them terribly. And since we were away from them for so long, I suffered from a feeling of guilt. Perhaps I should have stayed in southern California and played a more active role in their day-to-day lives.

I also missed having intellectual challenges. I missed working with clients and fellow consultants on problem solving. Discussing complex issues and figuring out solutions. Generating and sharing ideas, evaluating alternative strategies, and arriving at a decision. In short, I missed thinking.

While Wendy and I did think and make decisions during our drive, the issues we pondered were far from complex. Which road? Which campsite? Which bed and breakfast? Which hike? Truly a wonderful trip, but far from an intellectual challenge.

We're On Our Own

About six weeks before completing our driving trip, we learned that the Peace Corps had rejected my application. And I can truthfully say that we took this news pretty well. We didn't resent the personal commitment we had made to the Peace Corps—selling our home and Wendy's car, closing down her law practice and my consulting practice, and putting everything we owned in storage. Instead of looking back, we looked forward. We both agreed, "OK, if the Peace Corps won't have us, we'll create our own volunteer experience."

Sure, it would be somewhat more complicated to do it on our own. But why not? Certainly it would be more adventurous. And likely we'd learn a whole lot more. "Heck, we're committed. Let's do it."

In fact, we were especially enthusiastic about finding our own volunteer opportunity. As Wendy explained, "We now have a blank canvas on which we can paint any picture we choose."

We figured we'd stay in southern California for six months. In that time, we'd plan our move to Latin America and visit with Larry and Doug and our southern California friends. We signed a six-month lease on an apartment overlooking Newport's Back Bay. It was a great location, close to the boys and to our friends, right there on the bike trail and complete with decent exercise facilities. As all of our possessions were in storage, we rented furniture and borrowed dishes, pots and pans, silverware, and glasses.

Settled in our apartment, we immediately began planning our "next chapter." First we decided on the country in which we'd volunteer. Wendy suggested, "Let's go to South America rather than Mexico or Central America. Living in South America, we'd have the opportunity to learn about, and travel in, another continent."

"Yeah, that sounds fine to me," I agreed.

Researching each of South America's countries, we decided on Peru, for a number of reasons. First, Peru is centrally located on the continent. So from there, we could easily visit a number of other countries. And Peru is a poor country with many needs, so there, we'd likely have our choice of volunteer opportunities. And Peru has many indigenous people—twelve million of a total population of twenty-eight million. This would, no doubt, prove culturally interesting.

Lastly, Peruvians speak a beautiful Spanish. Unlike Chile, whose dialect is difficult even for Spanish speakers from neighboring countries to understand, Peru offers a very pure version of Spanish. As Wendy was then relatively new to the language, this factor was especially important. It was settled; we'd go to Peru.

The Peace Corps sends its volunteers to three months of training in the country where they will later work. That training includes an orientation to the culture plus training in the language. With this in mind, Wendy and I decided we'd begin our sojourn in Peru with a few weeks of language school.

And so, we searched, mainly on the Internet, for language schools in Peru. As we expected, we found the language schools to be centered in the larger cities. Lima certainly, and also Trujillo, Arequipa, and Cusco. Lima was out because we had no interest in living in a city of eight million people. Cusco was out because it was far too touristy. We favored Arequipa rather than Trujillo because of its location in southern Peru. From there, we'd be more centrally located on the continent, closer to Bolivia, Chile, and Argentina. All interesting places to visit.

An Internet search revealed three language schools in Arequipa. We wrote to all three and received a prompt reply from one and a slower reply from another. Each of the schools offered "home stay," that is, they'd arrange for us to live with a local family. While we feared just a bit for our loss of privacy, Wendy and I also appreciated that home stay would offer us a great orientation both to the language and the culture.

OK, settled then, we'd begin the South American chapter of our lives with a language school and home stay in Arequipa, Peru. We'd travel to Arequipa, stay in a hotel for about a week, and look in on all three language schools in that city. With that settled, we'd next turn our attention to potential volunteer opportunities.

With some online research, I learned of an organization called Asociación para el Desarrollo Empresarial en Abancay (ADEA) (Association for Entrepreneurial Development in Abancay). ADEA was a non-government organization (NGO) funded by the Belgian government. Its mission was to improve the economy in the town of Abancay and in the yet poorer surrounding region of Aprurímac in the Peruvian Andes.

ADEA had two specific functions. The first was to provide small loans to entrepreneurs, mainly artisans and farmers. The second was to consult to entrepreneurs. Hmmm … business consulting. Right up my alley. I began e-mail correspondence with a fellow named Danilo Córdova, the head of ADEA's consulting function. He told me that he could use my help in consulting to entrepreneurs.

I said to Wendy, "This opportunity with ADEA looks interesting. But I don't know what volunteer opportunities might be available to you in Abancay."

She said, "If the opportunity with ADEA is of interest to you, let's go to Abancay. I'm sure I'll find some volunteer opportunity there."

I sent Danilo an e-mail and told him we'd travel to Abancay to meet with him and explore the volunteer opportunity which he offered.

At the end of our lease period, we moved out of the Newport Beach apartment, parked the Landcrusier in a friend's garage, and purchased two one-way tickets to Arequipa, Peru. There we'd study Spanish for six weeks or so, then travel sixteen hours by bus to Abancay. In Abancay,

I'd meet with Danilo and, potentially, work with ADEA as a volunteer business consultant.

Our Move to Peru

Having deposited my old Landcruiser in our friends' garage on the central California coast, Wendy and I spent our last week in the USA driving a rental car. On March 5, we left our Newport Beach apartment and loaded the rental car with the gear we'd take to Peru. We each had a large backpack, a carry-on daypack, and a duffle bag.

We drove to a hotel near the Los Angeles Airport. Wendy waited at the hotel while I returned the rental car and walked back to the hotel. Over a quiet dinner in the hotel's restaurant, we toasted the beginning of our trip.

Following a good night's sleep, we showered and dressed. As per plan, I left an old shirt and a worn out pair of tennis shoes in the hotel room's closet. After breakfast, we checked out of the hotel and loaded our gear into the hotel's courtesy bus to the airport. About two hours later, we boarded our airplane.

During our American Airlines non-memorable dinner, Wendy asked, "Would you like a glass of wine."

I said, "Yes, it might help me sleep."

When the wine arrived, I suggested, "Let's toast to this new chapter in our lives. Just maybe we'll be in for quite an adventure."

Wendy replied, "Yes, and I believe we'll have an even greater adventure than we would have had if we were with the Peace Corps. Don't you think so?"

"Yes, I think you're right," I said.

"Maybe you'll someday write a book about our living in Peru," Wendy said. "Then it would literally become 'a new chapter in our lives.'"

"Yeah, maybe. Or maybe we'll write the book together," I suggested.

Wendy smiled and sipped her wine.

Following dinner, we tried watching the movie for a while. It was about as unmemorable as our dinner. I gave up after just a few minutes and began reading a book.

Wendy hung in there watching the movie. When it was over, she too began to read. After an hour or so, she grew sleepy. She closed her book and set it in the seat pocket in front of her. She pulled her blanket up from her lap and tucked it in around her shoulders.

A bit later I noticed that she had fallen asleep. I stared at her for a time just thinking, *Gosh, I'm a lucky fellow. Wendy is truly an amazing woman. How many women are this adventurous to step out into the unknown as we're doing? She closed her law practice, sold her home and her car, and put everything she owns in storage. Then she boarded an airplane to fly off to another continent for who knows how long? And what will she do when she gets there? We have no idea? Yeah, I'm a very lucky fellow.* ➤

Chapter 25

My First Peruvian Business Trip

IKNOW THAT I'M GETTING OUT AHEAD OF MYSELF. That I should save this story for my next book. But I'm ever so eager to tell you about my first Peruvian business trip. Here's what happened…

Following a six-week stay in Arequipa where we lived with a family and studied Spanish, Wendy and I traveled by bus to Abancay. There, we visited the ADEA office and met with Danilo. By the end of that day, he and I shook hands and decided to work together. Wendy set out in search of, and found, meaningful work in a children's after-school program.

I began my work with ADEA as a volunteer business consultant on May 16, and two weeks later went on my first Peruvian business trip. The event was a two-day workshop in Huanipaca, about a two-hour drive from Abancay. Saying it's a two-hour drive doesn't quite tell the story. Actually, it's about forty-five minutes on the paved highway and another hour and a quarter on an unpaved, mountainous road.

In the Peruvian Andes, there is very little private car ownership, thus one moves about by public transportation. So we hired a car complete with driver, and left from Abancay shortly before sunrise. Five of us, plus the driver, would make the trip in what Avis would call a mid-sized car. We had a laptop computer, LCD projector, rolled up flip chart paper, and a couple of boxes of supplies which we'd use in our workshop. And each of us had a backpack containing clothing and toiletries

From the ADEA office, we were three: Andrés, who would lead the workshop, plus Marleny and I who would assist. This particular workshop was specific to the local frijol (bean) growers. Hmmm ... I gotta admit, though my twenty-five years as a business consultant did include some work in agriculture, this was my very first assignment specific to beans.

Joining us in our early morning departure were an economist from the local university and a consultant who'd facilitate the meeting. As I was the tallest person in the group, I sat up front with the driver while the other four passengers crowded into the back seat. Seemed fine with me. I held the computer on my lap to protect it from the bumps we'd no doubt encounter.

Abancay is located at an elevation of about 7,500 feet. The surrounding high country is up about 11,000 to 17,000 feet. And so we climbed.

Gosh, it was unusually cold that morning! And foggy.

Up, up, higher and higher. Finally, about the time we went from the paved highway to the dirt road, we were above much of the fog and could see some of the snow-covered mountain peaks mixed with clouds. The window glass was as cold as ice.

After forty-five minutes or so, we turned onto the unpaved road. The scenery—what we could see of it through the intermittent fog—was beautiful. The mountain peaks were visible, but the canyon, way below, was deep in fog.

We bumped our way along and, just about two hours on the nose, arrived in Huanipaca. The town looked like so many other small, poor, mud-stained Peruvian pueblos. Huanipaca, which boasts a population of some two thousand, sits at an elevation of 10,900 feet. Man, it was cold stepping out of the car that morning! I should have worn my long underwear.

We drove to the Hotel Las Orquídeas on the far side of the Plaza de

Armas. There we'd drop our luggage before going to breakfast. The hotel was kind of a worn-out place consisting of a not-quite-pretty courtyard surrounded by a u-shaped building sporting a dozen or so rooms on two levels. Marleny had apparently stayed there before, since she immediately announced, "I'll take room number six."

Andrés and I got room number one. He claimed the bed on the left. Our room had a table and a chair. And two windows opening out to the courtyard. But no bathroom.

For a bathroom, we'd walk to the back of the courtyard where we'd find a potty with no lid, no seat, and no toilet paper. Not to worry though, I learned soon after arriving in Peru to carry toilet paper always. Oh yeah, a sink outside the bathroom, along the back wall of the courtyard, and a separate little shower house. Cold water, of course.

Marleny had ADEA's petty cash so she paid for our rooms. Andrés told me that our room cost was 10 soles per person, about $3.30 US Dollars. Yeah, maybe worth it. Maybe.

Going for breakfast, we walked through the typical, broken adobe storefront, stepped carefully down a one foot high, mud step, onto a mud-floored backyard filled with wood tables and chairs. Overhead was an enormous, blue canopy insuring shade. On this very cold morning, shade was the last thing we needed. With my shoes on the damp mud, my feet were especially cold.

"Mate de coca?"

"Sure, I'll have one. And make it hot."

After shivering through breakfast, we walked across the street to the municipal building—the center of most everything in Huanipaca. This building, where we'd conduct our workshop, looked like it might be a hundred and fifty years old. Maybe more. Large, adobe faced with multiple layers of concrete covered over with multiple layers of paint, each layer peeling so as to reveal a variety of colors beneath.

The building was surrounded by a fence and gate. There were about seven or eight steps up to the entrance. Two meeting rooms and three or four offices. We'd be in the meeting room on the right, the one nearest to the telephone room.

Huanipaca's phone system is typical of those in many pueblos of the Peruvian Andes. The town has just one phone line and just one phone. That phone is located in the municipal building. So if you want to call someone in Huanipaca, Señora Rodríguez for example, you simply dial the town's one and only phone number and ask for her by name. The phone operator, an unusually large fellow with an unusually large belly for a Peruvian, will then pick up his microphone and announce over the public address system that Señora Rodríguez has an incoming phone call. Then Señora Rodríguez will hurry over to the municipal building to receive her call.

Oh, don't worry, Señora Rodríguez will hear the announcement. The two large speakers mounted on a pole just outside our meeting room boast an enormous volume. The announcement will easily cover more acreage than does the town. How many calls? Oh, I guess we heard a dozen or so such announcements per day.

The outhouse was over in the corner of the front yard, just inside the surrounding wall. A concrete structure with two rooms, one with a potty (that's right, no lid, no seat, no paper). The other simply a hole in the middle of the floor plus an ever-dripping water pipe sort of rinsing things a bit. And wetting visitors' shoes as well.

We needed electricity for our computer and LCD projector. Certainly this old building wasn't originally wired for electricity. So the room's only light bulb, a dusty lonely soul, hanging by its wires from a beam on the ceiling, was powered by wires coming in through one of the room's few high windows.

Two of the local guys, seemingly in charge, brought in a roll of insulated wire. They first tried to capture electricity by stripping back insulation from the wires to the light bulb and also from the ends of their newly arrived wire. Neither they nor I could figure out why that didn't work, but it didn't.

Next, they dragged their wire via the front porch into the next room. There, they found an extension cord into which they could plug the wire tips from which they had removed insulation. A bit of masking tape to steady the whole affair and we had power for our laptop and LCD projector.

We, and everyone else, had to carefully step over the wire running across the front porch. Seems as though, in Peru, this sort of a set-up isn't all that unusual. For the next two days, folks would deal with this wire-beneath-their-feet just fine.

The Workshop

A dozen or so, most of them young frijol farmers, dressed in muddy jeans and sandals, drifted in slowly. The seminar got going at 11:00 AM, exactly an hour past our intended start time. Pretty typical. Luís, our facilitator, started with a bit of "Welcome all, how about introducing your-selves?" And so we did.

Andrés presented an overview of our two-day agenda. The rest of us listened and shivered from the cold. From time to time, we heard the loud-speaker blast notice of another incoming phone call.

Somewhere around late afternoon we broke for lunch. The same cold, mud-floored outdoor place where we had breakfast. Hot soup tasted great. Then the usual rice and a bit of meat—chicken, as I recall. Then back to the municipal building to resume our workshop.

The afternoon dragged by ever so slowly. As the sky grew dark and the air temperature changed from very cold to ice cold, the economist stood up to speak. He began by discussing a number of international economic factors, which were about two and a half kilometers over the heads of the jean-clad farmers.

I sat up straight and tall as he spoke about the Free Trade Agreement then being negotiated between the United States and Peru. He explained that some Peruvians, but not all, would benefit from the passage of the Free Trade Agreement. Generally, those who would benefit would be those along Peru's Pacific Coast where goods—generally, agricultural products and mined metals—could easily be shipped to the United States. Those who would not benefit would be the agriculturalists from the Andean pueblos, including the very one in which we were then shivering, where shipping to the coast and beyond was cost-prohibitive.

The economist then described a number of the "strong arm tactics" which the United States was using to remain the dominant party in the trade agreement. I felt somewhat uncomfortable about this "Big, Bad, USA" presentation. Though, in a strange way, I also felt privileged. It occurred to me that few Americans ever get the opportunity to sit in on such a ground-level view of what others thought of the United States as a trading partner.

We were ahead of schedule, and it seemed that we'd finish up about 7:00 PM, a full hour earlier than our intended stop time. But no such luck. Marleny and Andrés had a terrific surprise for us—two lengthy, unrelated, maxi-boring motivational films. The darkness grew colder. The hunger grew more intense. My enthusiasm for this adventure grew dimmer. The loudspeaker blared out notice of another incoming call.

Finally, mercifully, the motivational stuff concluded and we walked to that same restaurant for dinner. Entering in the dark, I missed the high mud step and landed, embarrassed but unharmed face down on the cold, mud floor. Dinner moved along quickly. I remember enjoying the hot mate de coca. Man, my feet were cold!

Off to the hotel and to bed. I put on pajamas and, still shivering, crawled under a mountain of covers. Andrés didn't bother getting undressed. He simply removed his shoes and crawled beneath the covers, clothes and all.

My shivering diminished a bit and I drifted off to sleep.

A Brighter Day

The next morning, the world looked and felt far better. Bright sunshine and much warmer. Even the mud floor in what was apparently the town's only restaurant seemed less cold. Breakfast and then back to the municipal building to resume our workshop. In fact, our workshop moved along nicely. More group exercises than lecture made for a far livelier day. A promised stop time at 1:00 PM turned into an actual 2:00 PM stop. And then a quick lunch. Yeah, at the same old place.

And where was the hired car whose driver had agreed to wait for us? Gone. Seems that, on this second day, there was another group meeting in the adjoining room, the room from which we had dragged in our electrical line. That meeting ended an hour before ours. So the driver of our hired car decided that, instead of waiting for us as he had agreed, he could get back to Abancay somewhat earlier, and perhaps with a higher fare, if he would simply abandon us and haul folks from the other meeting. So there we were, about 2:30 PM on Friday afternoon, without transportation back to Abancay.

"No problem," said my Peruvian co-workers. "We'll simply wait for some other car to come into town hauling some other people. The driver will be happy to take us back for the usual fare."

While I did find some comfort in their confidence, I still had some concern. OK, we'd wait. Come to think of it, what choice did we have?

Then, Andrés said, "I didn't like the food we had for lunch, so I ate very little. I'll walk to a store to find some fruit, or perhaps a can of tuna and some bread. Do you want to come along?"

I said, "Yes."

While eating tuna and bread, Andrés chatted with the fellow who ran store. Across from the store, I sat on a bench in the Plaza de Armas watching some boys kick a soccer ball. Then I heard Marleny call my name. There she was a block away, waving to me to come to her. I figured she had found us a ride back to Abancay. Yea, Marleny! I ran to the store to fetch Andrés. Then we both ran to Marleny and to our "rescue vehicle."

There, in the middle of the road, in front of the municipal building, was a late model pick-up truck parked facing away from us. Dark green. A Ford, I think. Up in the bed of the pick-up truck stood Marleny and a tall fellow whom I didn't recognize. On the sideboards of the truck's bed sat two other fellows whom I also didn't recognize. In the bed of the truck was a whole bunch of equipment. Backpacks, our computer and projector, plus large pieces of paper, from our meeting, rolled up into a tube. Plus a whole lot of luggage.

Apparently, the three guys in the bed of the truck were attendees from the meeting in the room next to ours. Through the truck's rear window, I could see two rows of seats. Not only were there four people in the bed of the truck, there were another six people seated inside, three in the front seat and three in the rear seat.

Andrés and I tossed our packs onto the pile in the bed of the truck and hopped over the tailgate. He wedged himself into a narrow standing space in the front of the truck bed beside Marleny and the tall fellow. There, he could hang onto the roof of the cab. I, the last aboard, had little choice. I plopped down in a seating position on the floor of the bed, facing forward, with my back against the upright tailgate. I stretched out my legs as best I could, some luggage beneath my legs, some on top of my legs and in my lap. I found the black nylon computer case and dragged it onto my lap to cushion the computer as best I could. I figured we were in for a bumpy ride.

Off we started, up the dirt road headed to the highway. I guess it was about 3:00 PM. The bumps were bad but not terrible. As this was a fairly late model truck, its shocks were, thankfully, in decent shape. This was particularly good news for me, for seated as I was, with my back against the tailgate and my bottom planted squarely on the floor of the truck's bed, I was especially vulnerable to bumps.

A far greater problem was the dust. Except for an occasional stream crossing, where the driver mercifully slowed down to minimize the bumps, the road was dry. So the truck kicked up a lot of dust. About 18 percent of that dust found its way into my eyes, ears and nostrils.

As Huanipaca, at an elevation of 10,900 feet, is in a valley, we had to climb to arrive at the highway. The higher we climbed and the later the hour, the lower the temperature. I think we climbed up to about 15,000 feet. The view down into the valley, across the canyon, and beyond to the snow covered peaks, was magnificent.

As I hadn't anticipated traveling in the bed of a pick-up truck, I wasn't wearing my jacket—just two cotton shirts, one short-sleeved and one long. So I was really cold. Cold, dust, and an occasional bang on my bottom and back. During one particularly painful moment, I actually asked myself, *What in the world am I doing here?* I can't remember if I asked myself that question in English or in Spanish. Or if I asked it silently or out loud.

Marleny, Andrés, and the tall fellow, all standing in front of the truck bed, were likely colder than I. While they weren't so troubled by dust, they had a continuous cold wind in their face.

The young fellow seated on the sideboard to my left asked me, "What country?"

I said, "I'm from The United States."

He asked, "What are you doing in Peru?"

I responded, "My wife and I have come to Peru to work voluntarily."

He asked me, "Do you like Peruvians?"

I assured him that, "Yes, I like Peruvians very much. Since moving to Peru, my wife and I have made many Peruvian friends."

I had been so engrossed in conversation that I only half noticed the cramp developing in my left leg. Almost unconsciously, I wiggled it around beneath two backpacks and found partial relief. We were nearing the end of our climb and would soon be on the paved highway.

When the truck stopped at the highway, it took me a while to unravel from beneath the gear on my lap and legs. It also took me a while to get my cold, cramped body to respond to my calls for action. Finally, and somewhat painfully, I was actually standing up beside the truck. This was the moment I had been looking forward to for a dusty, ice cold hour and a half.

Marleny, Andrés, and I, walked around to the front of the truck to thank the driver. This was the first time I saw other than the back of his head. We wished all aboard the truck a good weekend. They'd be traveling about three more hours to Cusco. Probably about an 8:00 PM arrival. I remember thinking how very cold the ride would be for the three guys in the back of the truck.

Marleny, Andres, and I stood beside the highway waiting for a somewhat empty car or truck. Traffic was light. We watched two or three hired cars, each with five or six passengers, drive by. Then, while my back was turned from the highway, I heard the screech of air brakes. Sounded like a truck was stopping. I turned and saw a large, red semi-truck. The big 18-wheeler was coming to a stop right in the middle of the highway.

The truck had an open bed trailer, the kind used for hauling gravel or coal, or durable crops like onions or carrots. Actually, I didn't care what the truck was hauling; I was far more interested in hopping aboard. And so were Marleny and Andrés.

Gosh, the cab was high! Four metal steps up to the door. We sent Marleny up first. Then Andrés. Then, from below, I passed the packs, computer, and the rest of our gear up to Andrés.

I climbed aboard to find Marleny and Andrés in the rear seat wedged in with all our gear. I plopped down on the passenger seat beside the driver. Gosh, we were up so very high! I could see all the world from where I sat.

I had acres of room and it was warm. I hadn't known this much comfort since I couldn't remember when.

The driver, a stern looking, but friendly, middle-aged man, pushed into first gear and the truck ground forward. Then, with a bit of a lurch, second gear. *Hey, this was fun,* I thought. All of a sudden, I was enjoying myself.

Down, down, down the winding highway to Abancay. A ride that would have taken us forty-five minutes in an automobile would take us over an hour in the big semi. Our driver explained, "One has to be careful to keep it on the road in the turns." That sounded like a pretty good idea to me. I liked this fellow. He had the right attitude.

I sat back and relaxed. This was a different kind of a feeling. Being up so very high, seeing the world this way. The smooth turns. The stiff suspension. A real roll-up window so I could adjust my own air flow. And a warm, dust-free environment inside the cab. Yeah, this was neat.

I remember thinking that if the driver were to turn to me and say, "I've got to deliver this load to Topeka, Kansas. How'd ya like to go along for the ride?" I would have jumped at the opportunity. Yep, life had certainly improved since I peeled myself out of the bed of the pick-up truck. I looked back and saw that Marleny and Andrés were both asleep in the back seat.

Arriving in Abancay, we thanked the driver and climbed down from the cab. We all wished each other a good weekend and went our separate ways, Marleny in a taxi and Andrés and I on foot. I had a thirty-minute walk to our apartment where Wendy would be waiting for me to go out to dinner. I thought briefly about taking a taxi, but I felt so energized that I decided to walk.

Entering our apartment, I dropped my pack on the floor and gave Wendy a kiss. I was about to ask her if I had time for a shower, but she spoke first, "Why don't you take a shower before we go to dinner?" ➤

About the Author

BILL BIRNBAUM lives in Sisters, Oregon, with his adventurous wife, Wendy, a red kayak and a well-worn pair of hiking boots. Yes, he still drives his old Landcrusier. And he's working on another book.

He also writes a blog called "Adventure Retirement." Check it out at: www.AdventureRetirement.com